Modern Psychotherapy And the Directed Daydream

by

Ken Alexander, MSP, FNCP (Ho

First Editi

THE SEEKER PUBLICATIONS

Published in Great Britain in 2003
by
'THE SEEKER' PUBLICATIONS
"Badgers' Brook"
4 Brook Edge, Moor Lane,
Brighstone, Newport,
Isle of Wight. PO30 4DP.

Cover Illustration by Keith English
Cover design by Liam Baldwin

Printed and bound in Great Britain by:

Olivers Printers Ltd
Cesar House, Eastwood Road
Bexhill-on-Sea, East Sussex, TN39 3PS

ISBN: 0-9539013-0-0

Summary of Contents

ACKNOWLEDGEMENTS

Every science has its own jargon and psychotherapy is no exception. It is not the purpose of this book to provide a definition of all the terms used. Indeed, I have done my best to avoid jargon wherever possible. However, in the event that I have lapsed into it at times, a few of the words and terms in common use have been given in the text for clarification and a better understanding while on other occasions it has proven necessary to use page footnotes. Most definitions have been taken from Charles Rycroft's *A Critical Dictionary of Psychoanalysis* a reference book which I have found most useful over the years and which I recommend as a very useful aid to the serious student of psychotherapy.
The quotations are reprinted by permission of The Peters Fraser and Dunlop Group on behalf of Charles Rycroft © 1968: First published by Nelson 1968. Published by Penguin Books Ltd 1972.

* * *

Bibliography

Rycroft. Charles. *A Critical Dictionary of Psychoanalysis.* Published by Penguin Books Ltd., (1973). First published by Nelson (1968).
Blythe, Peter. *Hypnotism: Its Power and Practice.* Published by Arthur Barker Limited (1971).
Desoille, Robert. *The Directed Daydream.* Published by The Psychosynthesis Research Foundation, PRF Issue No. 18 from a translation by Frank Haronian, Ph.D.(1966).
Alexander, Ken, FNCP, MNCH (Acc),FRC. *Analysis of Psychotherapy, Hypnotherapy and Orthomolecular Treatments carried out between 1974 and 1982 in England, Canada and the United States.* (First of a series of 3 reports submitted to the British Medical Association (September 1983).
Alexander, Ken, FNCP, MNCH (Acc), FRC. *Analysis of Psychotherapy and Orthomolecular Treatments carried out between 1987 and 1988 in England.* Last of a series of three reports submitted to the British Medical Association (May 1988).
Assagioli, Robert, MD.. *Self-Realisation and Psychological Disturbances.* Published by The Psychosynthesis Research Foundation, PRF Issue No. 7. (1961)
Jung, Carl Gustav. , *Approaching the Unconscious (From Man and His Symbols)* and *Memories, Dreams, Reflections,* First Published in Britain by Collins and Routledge & Kegan Paul, 1963.

* * *

Modern Psychotherapy and The Directed Daydream

by

Ken Alexander, FNCP, MNCH, MSP, FRC

INTRODUCTION

During 1996 and 1997, I was privileged and honoured to address many students of mysticism at Surrey University, Guildford, on the subjects of *Modern Psychotherapy* and Robert Desoille's *"Directed Daydream"*. The first part of my address on each occasion was given over to a brief definition of psychotherapy and the many techniques employed, whereas the second and final part not only defined *"The Directed Daydream"* technique but gave those who attended the opportunity to participate in two of the six themes which the Daydreams are intended to cover. Two main points arose from the discussions, which took place after each part of the programme, namely: the enthusiasm and interest of those who participated and the inadequacy of the time allocated to cover such an extensive science. At the close of the second and final part of the programme it was suggested that I might write a book which would not only cover the main points of each address but hopefully expand upon them by providing far more data than it was possible for me to condense into the sessions; several students expressed a wish to participate in special training courses covering the subject in depth. Unfortunately, at the point of time of writing this book I am not in a position to provide training programmes on such a scale although this is a possibility that I am keeping in mind for the future.

I would like to take this opportunity of thanking the many volunteers who participated in the first two Directed Daydreams. As I explained to them it was the first time that I had used the Daydreams with a group of people instead of the "one-to-one" basis usual in the therapy situation. However, from the feedback following our group work it would seem that the results proved to be none the less effective, possibly due in no small part to the fact that all the participants were mystics capable of visualisation to a high degree!

Of course, I can identify with any who find the subjects of psychology and philosophy intriguing. They first engaged my interest during my early teens and indeed have continued to do so ever since. I remember that, for a time, I was undecided as to whether I should enter the Church, or Social Work. Fortunately, I chose the latter and made what I believe now to have been the right decision for me, since the dogma associated with the former would have become increasingly difficult for me to sustain over the years. Having said that, one aspect of the Roman Catholic Church needs consideration, however, and that is *the confessional.* The unburdening of guilt by the confessor in secret to the priest is nevertheless a *positive process* inasmuch as it releases *negative* energy; which otherwise would react unfavourably upon the troubled one.

My early training was with Dr. H.B. Kedward, MB, Ch.B, MA, Trinity College Oxford and an excellent introduction it was too for which I am exceedingly grateful to Dr. Kedward. For a while I worked as a journalist, a *chosen* occupation, which came about through a certain well-meaning, cap-and-gown individual who taught English. However, as the choice was *his* and not *mine* it was not long before I left the typewriter, London and a journalistic career far behind me with the proverbial "speed that might easily have given that particular street of the capital city its name!"

I entered social work in 1954 and spent eighteen years meeting people from many walks of life who had to deal with all manner of real life problems, albeit not infrequently of their own making. To them also I am grateful because it was through my contact with them that I learned the value of *proper communication.* Frequently the sheer number of people requiring help, my *case-load*, dictated what time I could allocate to each individual. It was not surprising, therefore, that I decided to enter Private Practice where I believed that I could work on a one-to-one basis with clients in a less hurried and altogether 'case-load-pressure-free' atmosphere. This decision was helped also by a very vivid dream or vision I had wherein I was introduced by an angelic being to the Rainbow of Health, a rainbow of such delicate quality and exquisite hue that I was overawed. The angelic being invited me to thrust my hand into the rainbow's delicate, ethereal texture, which I did, after some initial hesitancy. Although no words were spoken I knew that my initial hesitancy had been acknowledged and understood, after which the impression was conveyed to my mind that I had partaken of a solemn rite and in so doing had pledged myself to healing work.

Having seen the value of hypnosis as a therapeutic aid in psychotherapy, I undertook a further period of training at the National College of Hypnoses and Psychotherapy, obtained a Diploma and later became a Licentiate Member of the National Council of Psychotherapists. After further study and a period in practice, followed by an examination, I was admitted to full membership of the National Council of Psychotherapists and my name duly entered on the Hypnotherapy Register, a register of competent practitioners from which referrals are made by the Council.

At this point I would like to emphasise the need for anyone thinking of entering private practice in either psychotherapy or hypnosis to undergo proper training and preferably gain some experience in the art of communication first, since that is what psychotherapy, indeed any form of counselling for that matter, requires of the practitioner because they are "talking cures". Mainly the person with the problem does the talking, while the therapist *listens* and *observes.* Therapy therefore requires of the therapist keen *observation,* which, in turn, requires *patience* and *alertness*. Whilst at times firmness is needed in directing a certain course which therapy should follow, it is usually done without any emotional reaction or display by the therapist. Sometimes the best results in a therapy situation depend upon the therapist's silence as much as anything.

Training usually involves practical work, or sessions, where each student takes on the role of therapist and patient in turn; that is in 'theraping' and 'being theraped', under the overall guidance of a qualified and experienced tutor. Such sessions are invaluable to the student because he gains vital experience but within a controlled framework affording him the opportunity of applying what he has learned and also enabling him to work through many of his own hang-ups which might otherwise occlude his ability as a therapist.

CHAPTER 1

Love

There is no difficulty that enough love will not conquer;
No dis-ease that enough love will not heal;
No door that enough love will not open;
No gulf that enough love will not bridge;
No wall that enough love will not throw down;
No sin that enough love will not redeem.
It makes no difference how deeply seated may be the trouble,
How hopeless the outlook,
How muddled the tangle,
How great the mistake,
A sufficient realisation of love will dissolve it all.
If only you could love enough
you would be the happiest and most powerful being in the world.
- Emmet Fox

Psychotherapy and Psychoanalysis

Psychotherapy, as suggested in the Introduction, could be described as a *talking cure.* It may or may not include *Psychoanalysis,* a term which is applied to discovering WHY a person reacts in a certain way and assumes an underlying reason for his illness, emotional reactions, neuroses, etc. That is, that he has an *unconscious* area of his mind that can react upon him producing undesired responses or effects. It is not always necessary to undertake psychoanalysis to effect a cure.

A colleague once summarised it like this: "Whereas a good Psychotherapist will summon help from a doctor or by ringing for an ambulance if a man falls and breaks his leg, a bad one will try to discover *why* the man fell!"

An article, originally written for the Healing Research Trust, entitled *Healing — Psychotherapy,* which appeared in the *Rosicrucian Beacon*, Summer issue 1993, Vol. 2, No. 3, pp 10-12, attempted to define psychotherapy and the many schools of thought contained within it. The author concluded that " ... There are many ... schools of thought - probably as many as there are psychotherapists!"

I shall not attempt, therefore, to describe the many schools of psychoanalysis and psychotherapy that exist. Usually a particular school takes its name from its founder or originator; thus we have Freudian, Eriksonian, Jungian, Adlerian schools of psychotherapy. Many modern psychotherapists may use a composite of the various forms, to which they will have added some practical ideas of their own gained through experience.

Psychotherapy may be either *individual* or *group*. It may be *superficial* or *deep*.

It may be *Interpretative*, *Supportive* or *Suggestive*. The term 'intensive' is applied to either the frequency of the client's attendances OR the zeal displayed by the therapist.

Every science has its own jargon and psychotherapy is no exception. It is not the purpose of this book to provide a definition of the terms used. Indeed, I hope to avoid 'jargon' wherever possible but in the event that I should lapse into it at times, a few of the words and terms in common use are given below for clarification and a better understanding of parts of this book. It may also prove necessary from time to time to use page footnotes. Charles Rycroft's *A Critical Dictionary of Psychoanalysis* (Penguin Reference Books) is a very useful aid to the serious student.

ABREACTION: The discharge of *Emotion* associated with and attaching to a previously *repressed experience.*

SUPPRESSION: The *Conscious*, voluntary *inhibition of activity.*

REPRESSION: The unconscious, involuntary, automatic defence mechanism.

RITUAL: Originally a religious or magical ceremony or procedure. In Psychoanalysis it is used to describe a form of *solitary behaviour* displayed by persons suffering *Obsessional Neurosis.* It is an attempt to reduce *Anxiety* by the carrying out of stereotyped series of actions. ("Counter Magic").

Looking Briefly at the Mind

It is said that the average person uses only about 5% of his potential of which the *conscious mind* uses some 10% and the sub-conscious, 90% of that 5%. Einstein stated that only 0.02% of mans' intellect is used. *How* do we use our minds?

If we look on the conscious mind as being the tip of an iceberg we may get a clearer idea. The conscious mind has to deal with our every day activities associated with our *survival.* It cannot overload itself so uses a sort of *Memory Library.* Into this goes all, repeat all, our experiences from birth until transition (death). It may also include *past-life* experiences, including the memory of the human race. Just as Libraries have sections, e.g. fiction, non-fiction, as well as various sub-classifications so also does the Memory Library. Further, our Memory is *infallible. Total Recall* is possible. This has been proved through *Hypnosis.*

Incidents in life are either happy, unhappy or, to quote a word used by a delightful old lady I met from the rural area of Sussex, "*middlin'* ". Put another way, incidents are pleasurable, painful or mediocre. If we experience too much pain our *Critical Censor* comes into play. This is a device to protect us (our Guardian, as it were), one function of which is to stop us going completely mad with pain by introducing *unconsciousness.* We black out. This sounds good but unfortunately the Critical Censor cannot tell the difference between *external* pain production and *internal.* Thus, if an outside signal triggers the black out mechanism, so can an aroused memory.

Pavlov's Dogs

Probably most people have heard of Pavlov's experiments. At meal times a bell was rung; eventually the ringing of the bell could cause the dogs to salivate. We can call the bell a trigger in the dog's memory, a *signal.*

In man, there is not only a first signal sensory system that he shares with other life forms but also a 'second signal system', which distinguishes him from the animals, the possession of *Language.* For example, the *word* "bell" can replace the sound of a bell. "The bell for lunch has sounded!" Language can be spoken, heard or read.

Pavlov's experiments and findings were subsequently validated by Ivan Smolenski's experiment, which showed that "when a dynamic stereotype is established in man in either of (his) two signal systems, a precise response can be obtained in the other signal system without prior conditioning".

Pavlov wrote: "In man, the word is both qualitatively and quantitatively a conditional stimulus which is incomparably broader in its application than those of animals." Man's second signal system, according to A.N. Leontiev " ... makes psychotherapy possible ... and provides the rich possibility of educating the psychic processes."

Robert Desoille makes a further point: "Just as the words of our language, which make up the second signal system, are capable of functioning as signals, so also can *visual images* or other suggested imagery. There is a strict bond between *words* and their images; the two are inseparable. Experiments demonstrate conclusively that if a subject thinks a word, its verbal image is very frequently accompanied by other images ... usually of a visual character but sometimes olfactory, auditory and motor imagery, all of which being closely linked to the first system, are also evoked. All of the images, which can be evoked by a word, can also, in their turn, function as signals, thereby supplementing the second, characteristically human, signal system. This fact is extremely important, for in it lies both the explanation of how psychotherapy acts and the justification for its use."

If we can now return to what was said earlier about the Critical Censor, we see that there is a two-way passage between the present and the past, the NOW and the THEN, which is presided over by our Critical Censor. He can be over-zealous and keep or retain too painful incidents "down under" but he cannot stop their reacting upon us. All that is needed is a "trigger", which may take the form of a word, a visual image, a sound, a smell or any combination of these to restimulate the cell-memory associated with an original unpleasant experience and it can react upon us with or without our conscious knowledge. It means too that with the aid of therapeutic techniques we have access to this area and the capability of "defusing" a potentially explosive situation.

In my practice I used many psychotherapeutic methods but the main ones were *Free Association*, *Hypnosis* and *The Directed Daydream,* and to a lesser degree, *Implosive Therapy*. These will be discussed further in the next Chapter.

CHAPTER 2

An interior man will make more impressions on hearts by a single word animated by the spirit of God, than another by a whole discourse which has cost him much labour and in which he has exhausted all his power of reasoning.

Louise Lallement. (1587-1635)

In the last Chapter we discussed the mind and concluded that it has an outer conscious level which we can call the reasoning or thinking mind or analyser. There is also an inner level or memory storehouse, which files both pleasant and unpleasant memories of our experiences. Our pleasant memories can usually be recalled fairly easily as these are placed closer to the surface whereas very bad experiences containing pain of whatever kind, emotional, mental or physical, are placed in the deeper, darker recesses which we could term the 'dungeon' of the mind. All experiences are presided over by our *Critical Censor* or outer Guardian whose purpose is to monitor our experiences. If an experience is painful then the Critical Censor or Guardian will suppress the experience, cast it into the dungeon in his effort to preserve a state of harmony. All thought is *energy* and suppressed thought is no exception. Thoughts depend upon stimulation, usually from external stimuli. If we are engaged in pleasurable activity and the energy involved in that pursuit exceeds that of our stored or suppressed energy then we feel happy. If the external stimulus is less than our accumulated suppressed energy we may feel unhappy, sometimes very unhappy. Unresolved situations we may lazily hand over to the Guardian with the command to forget them, yet they may be causing us emotional pain or physical discomfiture. The Guardian is not concerned with our motives but will obey the command to 'forget' because his function is one of forgetting. Forgetting unfortunately does *not* stop *encysted energy* from affecting our moods; we may not be aware of the incident but the energy is there affecting us.

There are, additionally, other areas of the Mind available to us under certain circumstances: there is the Higher Consciousness or super-consciousness which I think of as being the *potential capability into which we shall ultimately grow, the Mind of Future Man or Higher Man.* There is also the *collective unconscious* to which Jung refers; this contains the regulator of bodily functions, racial memory and the source of certain of our intuitive faculties.

In the last Chapter we saw that psychotherapy is really a talking cure and that there are many schools of psychotherapy, many methods of releasing both rational and irrational fears through *communication.* Sometimes by various devices the therapist may be able to help his client release a great deal of "encysted" energy in the process which is called *abreaction,* or the discharge of *emotion* associated with and attaching to a previously *repressed* experience.

Before we proceed any further, however, there are some important and fundamental statements that I wish to make and which are based upon my experience over the years. The first is that we are all searching for *truth* whatever stage in our evolvement we have reached. *Truth* is the business of making the unknown *known.* Inasmuch as psychotherapy seeks to find the *cause* of a person's irrational behaviour, to release that person from the *unknown* or 'forgotten' episodes that can affect him, by making them known, it represents a quest for truth. For example, when a person feels *depressed* he feels that he is under great heaviness that is pressing down upon him, obscuring any chance of enjoying life. He has known periods of happiness and therefore is able to compare his present unhappy state with them and realises that all is not well. He hopes that the therapist will help him regain some happiness by lifting him out of the depression. Before seeking such help he may have been battling alone for weeks, months or even years. His request for help is an admission of *truth* that he wishes to overcome whatever it is that is causing his problem. If the motivation of the therapist is right, he too wishes to see his client achieve a better state, then he too is seeking *truth.* Thus, there is now the *combined* or allied quest for truth shared by the client and therapist. 'Two minds are better than one' as the saying goes; two minds that are united in the quest for *truth.* Rather than attempt to explain in detail the principles of the various psychotherapy techniques I propose giving illustrations, actual case histories, which may give a clearer picture of how a particular method or technique works.

On this matter of *truth* the following case history is perhaps the best illustration I can give:

Case Ref: T1/76

Mrs T, a divorced woman with no children, was referred to me by a local Welfare Organisation. She had not worked since losing the use of her legs some three years previously following an accident and had been confined to a wheel chair since the accident. She sought help in reducing cigarette smoking, which had developed into the chain habit and was not only causing her coughing but also financial problems.

As this was my shortest therapy session, requiring no further consultations, I have reported as accurately as possible what took place. Normally with folk seeking help in overcoming the smoking habit, I would have used *hypnosis* but her aggressive attitude made relaxation on her part virtually impossible. Whatever techniques I tried to employ she attempted to reject scornfully. She obviously had a great deal of anger that she wanted to vent. When there was a long enough pause in one of her vitriolic verbal onslaughts I asked her: *"Why do you feel the need to smoke so much?"* I repeated this question to her over and over, any irrelevant and venomous remarks made by her being entirely ignored. She finally retorted: "Wouldn't YOU smoke all day if you were in a wheel-chair all day?"

As this was the first communication, which she had made relevant to the problem about which she had consulted me, I answered:

"I cannot say because I have never had to be in a wheel-chair any day".

A silence elapsed following which she asked quite quietly: "Yes, but IF you had to be in a wheel-chair, wouldn't you feel like smoking all day?"

The reply I gave her was: *"I have smoked but cannot say whether or not I would have smoked more if I had been sitting in a wheel-chair"*.

With great venom she then said: "It's all right for you, you can walk. Do you think I would be in this ------- chair if I could walk?"

I said: *"I don't know"*.

In great anger she cried: "You think I can walk, I suppose".

I did not answer whereupon she changed her statement to a question.

"Do you think I would waste my time sitting in a wheel-chair all day if I could walk?"

I replied that *I* did not know.

She retorted: "Of course, I didn't expect you to answer *that*. Well, let me tell you that I have not walked for three years and I've been stuck in this chair all that time".

I allowed the silence to build up. Finally she felt compelled to break it by asking: "Do you think I can walk *now*?"

I replied: *"I do not know. Can you walk* ***now****?"*

"I have just told you that I haven't walked for three years and been stuck in this chair, doesn't that answer you?"

To which I replied that three years ago something had happened which had stopped her from walking *at that time* but as to whether she could walk now only she could answer that.

At that point she stood up from her wheel chair and unsteadily at first made a few steps towards me.

"I *can* walk", she said.

She could walk! The amazement on the face of the nurse who brought her in was something I shall never forget, nor the joy on the client's face as she left the room under her own steam. I feel that the method, which I had employed instinctively, was merely answering factually every question she had put to me and the *truth* had set her free. Whether or not she ever gave up or reduced smoking I do not know but I was told that she had continued to make good progress with walking and had taken up an occupation again. She had been surrounded by people whom she had paid for three years to look after her and probably had received too much insincere sympathy.

Mr X Mr Y

This particular case history illustrates something important about *communication*. Perhaps it would have been more accurate if I had described psychotherapy as being a *communication cure* rather than a talking cure. There is a marked difference between the two.

Consider for a moment the drawing above which represents two people, Mr. X and Mr.Y who are about to engage in an exchange of ideas. Mr X has a clear picture in his mind of what he wants to convey to Mr Y. Let us call his thoughts "A". Ideally he would like to transfer his thoughts directly, telepathically as it were, to Mr Y so that there can be no misunderstanding. However, he cannot do this so has to rely on his using the right words instead. If he is an articulate person his effort will closely approximate to his original thoughts "A" but even then will not exactly duplicate them. Let us call his effort "a" (little A). If Mr Y is equally articulate as Mr X he will have received "a" and then has to search his own memory for *his* understanding of what "a" means. Having done this he then needs to formulate his reply to Mr X. If both men are of the same nationality, from the same region, with the same background, equal understanding of the subject then Mr Y 's initial reply should be a fairly close approximation to the information expected by Mr X. Suppose we call Mr Y's understanding and thoughts on the subject "B", by the time he has formulated this into words, however, the communication back to Mr X will probably be something less than "B" and so we will call it "b" (little B). So more questions and more answers from one to another may take place over a period of time until Mr X is reasonably satisfied that Mr Y has understood him. The position becomes more complicated if both men come from different backgrounds even if fellow countrymen. Supposing too that Mr X has a greater understanding of the subject than Mr Y, or Mr Y is hard of hearing! It is no wonder that there are so many misunderstandings in this world of ours. Even trying to formulate these thoughts and convey them through the *written* word convinces me that *communication* can be quite exhausting!

Psychotherapy is, I believe, an exact science and proper communication between the client and therapist is essential. The therapist has to be observant, alert, always mindful that behind what a client may *say* are those unspoken thoughts which are in his mind which may well originate from the *occlusions,* past incidents of which he is no longer cognisant. Sometimes one psychotherapy method or technique may need to be abandoned in favour of another to bring the incident into the conscious realisation of the client. In this connection *hypnosis* may be the best method to employ.

Whatever technique I have used, however, invariably I have asked the client: "Have you had any significant dreams since our last session?" *Spontaneous Dreams* can be the client's way of working something out and it often proves helpful to go through his dreams with him. Dreaming can also be *induced* under hypnosis: " ... between now and the next time we meet, you are going to have a dream. You are dreaming either while you are going to sleep, while you are asleep, or when you are waking up. But what you are dreaming is revealing in some way, part of the problem you have been having. Because the dream is important, when you are waking up you are remembering *every detail* of it very clearly and because the dream is so vivid you will realise its importance and be able to tell me all about it next time we meet..."

Sometimes I have induced dreaming *during* hypnosis: " ... you are now in hypnotic time and therefore you can dream for as long as you like but in *actual time* (and that is the time I am in) you are dreaming for sixty seconds. So, when I say the word 'dream!' you are dreaming for as long as you want in *hypnotic-time* but when I say 'Stop!' your dream (or dreams) will have ended and you are remembering what you have dreamt..."

It is, of course, important that the client does recall his dream so that it can be discussed with the therapist and the client is able to identify its relationship to his problem.

In the last Chapter I said that in my practice I used many psychotherapeutic methods but the main ones were *Free Association, Hypnosis* and the *Directed Day-Dream*, also to a lesser extent, *Implosive Therapy.* I will now attempt to explain what these are:

Implosive Therapy

I first came across Implosive therapy some thirty years ago when I was in the United States. It is used to help overcome phobic anxiety. However, no attempt is made to discover the underlying *cause* of the fear or anxiety and psychoanalysis is confined to the recognition that a problem exists and there is no attempt to challenge its validity. The client is directed to imagine himself in the situation he fears and this process is repeated again and again until the client can face the situation without anxiety. By repetition the fear loses its energy; basically the mind becomes bored with it! Sometimes running through a fear as few as four or five times is enough while at other times many sessions are needed.

When I first discussed the method with a Professor of Psychology who favoured its use, my first question to him was: "Does the client subjugate one anxiety to another?" His reply was that he did not believe so. My next question was: "What proof, if any, could be offered that psychosomatic effects of the original anxiety clear themselves?" He was unable to offer any statistical evidence in support of his belief, of course, and admitted quite frankly that many clients' presenting symptomology sometimes masked the nature of their real problems, for example, where a guilt factor was involved, it was quite probable that this would remain undiscovered with implosive therapy. Admittedly, and on this we were in complete agreement, there was a danger of this occurring where other methods were used, particularly certain forms of hypnosis which subjugated symptoms and made no effort to discover *why* the client *needed to* confront the therapist and, indeed, his world, with those symptoms. So far as "follow-ups" were concerned we agreed that it is probably easier to follow-up on those clients who had terminated therapy before the treatment had been completed than those who had "stayed the course" because such an approach itself might sow seeds of doubt in the client's mind by implication; that a possibility existed that an improvement or 'cure' could be merely a temporary remission. Further, on this question of follow-up, Jung once remarked that quite by chance he had met, years after, one of his former clients who had terminated therapy and whom Jung had regarded as a 'failure', psychotherapeutically speaking; he was surprised therefore to be thanked by the client for all he had done in putting him on the right road to recovery! Thus, we concluded that *Implosive Therapy* was a method of psychotherapeutics that could be used effectively under certain circumstances and that the initial consultation with the client was all-important in deciding whether or not it was the best method available for that particular client!

The initial consultation is important in many ways but this will be looked at in more detail later. In the matter of *implosive therapy* I do know that it can be effective with certain fears of a *rational* nature but I am not enthusiastic about its use where there are irrational fear situations requiring deeper therapy. Below is a case history of its effective use:

Case Ref. L2/74

This client was an actor by profession. Periodically he was required to make cross Atlantic trips but because of a real fear of an air disaster occurring he had made all such crossings by ship. He wondered whether hypnosis could be used to help him overcome what he described as his "irrational fear of flying". Although I taught him some relaxation exercises, I did not induce hypnosis. Instead, I used implosive therapy because I did not regard his fear as being an irrational one. After all is said and done, it is *not* natural for man to fly but trans-Atlantic airline crossings are undertaken so often by so many of us in this day and age that they are considered to be commonplace. Whilst the client was in a relaxed state following some neck rolling exercises and a hand concentration exercise, he was asked to visualise a blue sky, which he did quite easily. I then asked him to see, in that sky, an aeroplane that was coming in to land. Again he did this without any difficulty. He was taken through the safe landing of this aircraft and subsequently the disembarkation of the passengers including the unloading of their luggage from the aircraft's hold. He described the subsequent refuelling and checking of the aircraft by the ground crew maintenance men. Subsequently he was asked to describe the departure lounge and gate at the airport, to see himself boarding the aircraft, being shown to his seat by a stewardess, fastening his seat-belt when the aircraft's engines were ready for take-off. He went through all the experience of "take-off", watched the ground 'fall away' as the aircraft climbed and flew into and above the clouds. Ultimately, after what appeared to be an enjoyable flight, the aircraft reached its destination and he was able to describe the landing and his disembarkation with his fellow passengers. In all, he went through the whole experience *seven* times. Some days later he made his first actual flight and explained to me that whilst he had experienced the 'butterflies', which even many experienced travellers suffer, he had been overjoyed to find that he had not been thrown into a panic. Perhaps he was as much afraid of this, of being unable to control panic in front of his fellow passengers, as he was of flying and thus, suffered both rational and irrational fear.

I have used implosive therapy with many other clients over the years quite effectively but the above example has been selected as it illustrates the technique well.

In the next Chapter illustrations of the use of other techniques will be shown.

* * *

CHAPTER 3

"In the healing context, hypnosis is precisely the *opposite* of one person imposing his will on another. Rather, hypnosis means trying to impose your *own* conscious desire to be well upon your *own* body and mind. Certainly there is a therapist involved but in perspective, all the therapist is doing is helping the client achieve some goal which the *client* desires."
B Joan Amer on *Hypnosis* in "Natural Healing".

In the last chapter we looked at *Implosive Therapy*, one of the techniques used in Psychotherapy. We will now examine another technique, an effective working 'tool' of psychotherapy, *Hypnosis.* Its uses are extensive; for example, it can be used to overcome bad habits such as smoking, over-eating and other excesses and it can be used in so many other ways too, for example, in helping to overcome various phobic conditions, nervous reactions such as blushing, nail-biting, shaking, stammering, also insomnia, examination nerves (including driving tests). It enables the therapist to discover the cause of the client's problem (s) and can be used to produce *abreaction* (a discharge of emotion associated with and attaching to a previously repressed incident in the client's life).

Many clients are afraid of 'being hypnotised', fearing that the therapist may induce a state of unconsciousness or that, in what they consider to be a reduced state of awareness, they may be instructed to perform actions or say things over which they have no control. Probably science fiction books and films and the stage-hypnotist are responsible for having instilled such fears. Thus, at the initial consultation the therapist needs to explain, if he decides that hypnosis is the technique he will employ, that these fears are unfounded, that hypnosis is a state of relaxation achieved through the co-operation of the client with the therapist; that it is a *consent state.* By resisting the suggestions that are made a client merely shows that he is unable to relax properly and brings into question his confidence and trust in the therapist.

I do not propose looking at the various *induction* methods used, nor considering *how* hypnosis works. It would take far more space than can be allocated in this book. Whatever induction method is used, from the simplest eye-fixation technique to the use of complex rotating wheels accompanied by colour and sound, all have one thing in common and that is the by-passing of the subject's *analyser* or *critical censor.* If we take a simple illustration, suppose I ask a client to stare at a pendulum which I proceed to swing rhythmically in front of his eyes and to keep his eyes fixed on that pendulum. Assuming he is prepared to co-operate, his analyser is at once engaged in performing the simple command of tracking the pendulum. Now suppose I introduce a second command: "Whilst concentrating on tracking the swing of the pendulum as it moves from side to side, I would like you to breathe deeply and evenly, breathing in to the count of five, holding the breath for a count of five and then breathing out to a count of five". This additional command is now imposing too much on the analyser or critical censor, which prefers to deal with one thing at a time. We may now add additional commands that the client's analyser will not be able to reject because it is already "tied up". "Because you are keeping your eyes fixed upon the pendulum as it swings from side to side, you may find your eyes becoming tired and it is quite natural that your eyes may become tired as you are watching the pendulum swinging from side to side, side to side, side to side. And because you are breathing so rhythmically you are feeling very relaxed and with each breath you are taking you are feeling more and more relaxed, more and more relaxed and more tired with each swing of the pendulum. As your eyes are feeling more and more tired with each swing of the pendulum and with each breath you are taking, so your eyelids are feeling heavier and heavier and soon your eyes are so tired and your eyelids are so heavy that your eyes are closing, your whole body is relaxing, and you are drifting into the deepest, most pleasant, relaxed state you have ever experienced.

In his book, *Hypnotism, Its Power and Practice,* Peter Blythe explains: "once the critical censor of the mind is by-passed and the subject allows things to happen, we have the condition known as *hypnosis"*. He defines hypnosis as " ... a consent state of physiological relaxation where the subject allows the critical censor of the mind to be by-passed to a greater, or lesser, degree. When the critical censor is by-passed to a greater degree ... the subject has reached the deepest known level of hypnosis and is a *somnambule*, the equivalent of a sleep-walker; and if it is only slightly by-passed the subject is referred to as being at a hypnoidal level.

It is sometimes necessary to demonstrate to the client that he has, in fact, achieved a state of hypnosis or relaxation and this can be done through hand levitation. After the induction, I ask the client to imagine that tied to the index finger of his left hand is a small balloon filled with hydrogen. I then ask him to see this balloon gently lifting into the air and as it lifts gently upward so he can feel a pleasant pull on the string attached to his index finger and now the index finger is lifting upwards as it gently lifts with the balloon. I then suggest that there is a wonderfully light feeling in his whole hand, which is wanting to float upwards with the pull of the balloon and because he is relaxing so well he is allowing his hand and his whole arm to float gently upwards with the balloon ... Usually the client's hand and arm will raise several inches and at that point I ask him to open his eyes. Of course, when he sees that his hand and arm have lifted and is not conscious of having lifted them he is usually satisfied that he has achieved a state of hypnosis or relaxation.

Many people who enter the healing professions believe that they themselves must be seen to be completely fit and free of all weaknesses, physical or psychological. However, one of the most successful hypnotherapists I have met who specialised in helping people overcome the smoking habit was, himself, a chain-smoker! He actually lit up a cigarette after having successfully induced hypnosis and continued to enjoy his inhalations of smoke throughout the session:

"...So you are finding as you are relaxing now, that deep, deep down inside you, you know that you can do what you wanted to ... you have that extra surge of willpower allowing you to be what you wanted to be - a permanent and lasting non-smoker and you know that nothing and no-one could ever tempt you to smoke again..."

Deepening techniques rely upon a trigger or signal, which the hypnotherapist uses. The trigger or signal may be a physical one whereby the hypnotherapist physically lifts his client's arm to demonstrate the achievement of relaxation by the client or it may be a verbal trigger or signal. The late Dave Elman whose methods have been copied or adapted by many hypnotherapists, doctors and dentists used the verbal trigger 'now':

"... In a few seconds time I am going to say the word 'now' and when I say the word 'now' in a few seconds time, every muscle in your body is relaxing. Yes, even the smallest muscle from the top of your head, all the way down to your fingertips and the tips of your toes.

"Every last ounce, every last drop of tension is going out of your body and your body is sinking into the chair completely and utterly limp. In fact, your body is so relaxed and so limp ... it is almost as if your body is no longer a part of you. This is a very pleasant feeling and because it is so pleasant you are forgetting all about your body. You are letting go and going into the deepest, most relaxed state you have ever been in.

"Now. And *now* let every muscle in your body relax. That's good. And *now* let your body sink down into the chair completely and utterly limp ..."

The use of word signals, however, requires sensitivity to the needs of the individual client. For example, to suggest to a client that his or her body is relaxing and feeling *heavier* and *heavier* can be a complete turn-off to the client who is seeking help in weight reduction! Most of us are sensitive to words like *pain* and the use of such a word by the unthinking hypnotherapist can jerk a client right out of a relaxed state! The use of "discomfiture" in the place of "pain", however, seems to be acceptable to most of us.

The following case histories demonstrate how effective hypnotherapy can be:

Case History A4/75

A local Health Clinic referred this client; a widow aged 70, to me. She was suffering pains in the left side of her breast extending to the armpit and spine. Extensive investigations had been carried out by her GP and subsequently by Consultants from the Hospitals to which she had been referred; the condition had been diagnosed as *inter-postural neuritis.* Pain-killing drugs had been prescribed but had provided very little relief from pain. Osteopathy and Massage had also proved of little value to her and she sought hypnotherapy as a last resort!

The initial consultation, lasting just over an hour, was devoted mainly to obtaining as much background information as possible about her life, hobbies, interests, etc. She was taught two relaxation exercises, one of which enabled her to enjoy considerable relaxation and during that time *hand levitation* was achieved without any difficulty. A further appointment was made for the following week.

She arrived punctually, advised me that there had been a slight improvement in her condition following her consultation the previous week and assured me that she had been spending considerable time each day performing the relaxation exercises which I had taught her. *Hand levitation* was achieved again with no difficulty and a *deepening* technique subsequently used.

During hypnosis she relived many incidents in her past of which two appeared to have a direct relation to her problem. The first was connected with a financial matter which had given her a great deal of anxiety (guilt) while the second involved a train journey which she had undertaken alone, encumbered with much luggage, which she had been forced to carry herself as there was no porter available at the railway station. Whilst reliving, re-enacting these two incidents there was a great deal of tension released through tears and convulsive sobbing.

After bringing her back into the "now" at the end of her hourly session, a further appointment was made for the following week.

Again she arrived punctually. She told me that the improvement in her condition had continued since her last session, with the pain having diminished and restful sleep achieved with the use of sedatives. She seemed very pleased to get back into "session" and again relived the two incidents already referred to. However, she was able to relate both incidents to her problem, which was her inability to travel, with the result that she had been unable to visit her children although invited to do so on many occasions. The earlier incident on the train had, in fact, caused her pain due to muscular tension trying to cope with too much luggage and also caused mental anxiety that she might not be able to cope and might miss her connecting train. The financial matter was connected with her family and involved the holding on to something that she felt was wrong (something of financial value which she should have passed on to her children but did not do so). The two incidents were very much related in her mind and when she subsequently resolved not to hang on to the valuables but hand them over to her children and to visit her children for this purpose, the pain in her breast, shoulder and back lifted immediately! She decided to accept the invitation her children had extended to her to spend a holiday with each of them in turn (in the North of England) and further resolved to take only a small suitcase with her since she had ample money to buy anything else she might need whilst away.

At the end of this session she was asked to let me know when she would like to see me again following her visits to her children.

Conclusion

She telephoned me to tell me that she was still up North with her children and thoroughly enjoying herself (this was a month after the session). She said that she had been entirely free of pain since her last visit to me. She saw no need for any further hypnotherapy sessions. She added that she was still performing the relaxation exercises daily.

As far as I am aware there has been no recurrence of the problem from which she had suffered many years and feel sure that had there have been she would have got in touch with me.

*   *   *

Case History D1/79

This client aged 41, was referred to me by her GP. She had been widowed four years and living alone since her husband's death; there having been no children of the marriage. Presenting symptomology: hypertension (high blood pressure), overweight, tension in her neck and left forearm. Treatment had comprised medicines prescribed by her doctor and some desultory attempts to lose weight by dieting.

Hypnosis was induced at the initial consultation and a deepening technique used after induction. After dealing with one or two seemingly minor problems, this client was directed to relive the most recent attack of hypertension, which she did. Several similar incidents were worked through and she was then asked to relive the very first time she had experienced the symptoms. She immediately relived the time when her husband was dying (she had nursed him at home). She related that she was under *great pressure* at that time and that she had had every reason to be. It seems that the diagnosis of high blood pressure was made several months after her husband's death; formerly she had enjoyed very good health all her life. She remarked, following her session that she could see why she might have had high blood pressure during the time when she was nursing her husband but could see no reason for having it afterwards!

Conclusion

The blood pressure and other symptoms disappeared after only two hypnotherapy sessions except for the overweight problem. She returned to work and the routine of her new life with an adjustment of her eating habits brought about the desired weight reduction quite quickly.

*   *   *

Case History A3/81

This young woman was referred to me by her GP. She was married with two sons ages 9 and 10. There had been frequent marital quarrels, with her husband leaving her on more than one occasion but returning after absences of a few days. Her father, of whom she had been very fond, had died seven years ago and this loss had been restimulated by the recent death of her brother-in-law aged 28. Marriage had been fraught with many difficulties including sexual incompatibility as a result of which she had become frigid. Presenting symptomology: headaches with feelings of depression also frequent heavy colds with aching limbs, digestive troubles and feelings of nausea. She was also smoking about forty cigarettes a day because of "nerves". Her doctor had prescribed *Melleril* and previously she had been on courses of Valium and Librium over many years.

At the initial consultation there was an initial block to hypnosis induction because she was unable to create mental image pictures. Much time was spent in seeking the cause of this blockage, which turned out to be an incident in early childhood when she had felt *bad* (ill) but had been told by her mother that there was nothing wrong with her "everything bad was in her imagination". Once this block had been removed therapy was able to proceed and hypnosis was induced easily. Over prolonged therapy she relived three abortions and much distress suffered during her first pregnancy when she had strong fears, possibly with some justification, that her husband was having an affair with another woman. The abortions, which she had undergone, however, had conflicted with her religious principles and although there was by now a marked improvement in her mental and physical health, she was still quite unable to respond to her husband's advances. At this stage, as further hypnotherapy sessions were yielding little change in her attitude to sex I decided to follow an intuitive 'hunch' and referred her to a colleague who practised massage with the result that after two or three body massages she was able to tolerate physical contact again.

Conclusion

Although considerable improvement had resulted from her psychotherapy and hypnotherapy sessions with me, the switch to *physical* treatment seemed to provide the right treatment for her at the time, increasing her tolerance to *feeling*. I maintained close liaison with both her GP and the Physiotherapist to whom I had referred her and can report that all presenting symptomology had cleared and she was able to reduce her doses of Melleril, finally dispensing with the drug altogether after two months. She was also able to reduce her cigarette smoking from about 40 a day to 15. Some months later she decided to see me again but this time for hypnosis to assist her in overcoming the smoking habit altogether!

* * *

Case History H.1/88

This client, a young married woman with two daughters ages 4 and 2, was referred to me by her GP Presenting symptomology: Quick tempered, irritation with her eldest daughter, headaches, catarrh, heavy menstrual pains and accompanying bouts of depression. Treatment before being referred to me had been confined to tranquillisers and pain depressant drugs.

Mild hypnosis was used at the first session to help her relax and also as an aid to analysis. After the second session she was able to relax quite well and the *Free Association* technique was used thereafter with good results. At one or two subsequent sessions when some difficulty was again encountered in getting her to relax, therapy was switched back to hypnosis. Not infrequently it was found that she had *current* problems, which she was encouraged to discuss. She was able to formulate plans for dealing with the current problems in this way and having arrived at her decisions was then able to go into a relaxed state; this also had the effect of increasing her self-confidence. Several incidents in her past were relived with a release of emotion and tension. She had been a fat child whilst at school and had been teased both there and at home. She was later able to relate pregnancy with weight gain and temporary loss of her attractive figure, which she felt accounted for her unhappiness during pregnancy, and her dislike of her eldest daughter. This client was very much in love with her husband and relived many happy incidents in their life together before the arrival of their first baby. She felt that she had resented the child's intrusion.

There was considerable improvement in the client's health at this point of time but although symptoms such as catarrh and headaches had cleared she was not fully free of bouts of irritation and menstrual difficulties.

She continued with therapy and at the next session relived an incident where a baby was crawling on a hearthrug towards an electric fire. She described the rug, the baby's position, the red glow of the fire, someone asleep in the room. She was horrified when the baby thrust a hand into the fire. She described the smell of burning flesh and how the sleeping person had leaped up from the chair and had picked up the baby. During the time that the client was reliving this incident I was fascinated to watch one of her hands which had screwed up from the finger tips to the palm and was jerking convulsively; tears were streaming from her eyes but she made no *sounds* of sobbing although her body was quite rigid. It later became apparent that the person who picked the baby up was her father and he was making loud "shushing" noises to stop the baby crying. The whole incident was described in very fine detail but the interesting thing was that she would not *identify the baby with herself.* (It was quite evident from my observation that she and the baby were one). Subsequently, as therapy proceeded and she recalled the incident over and over, she eventually identified herself with the baby from which point on there was a rapid improvement. She said that this incident was when she was eighteen months old and since then she had experienced a feeling of remoteness from herself, which had made her irritable and depressed. She was subsequently able to take responsibility for herself and her family and with great benefit to her home life.

Conclusion:

Therapy continued for two further sessions during which other incidents in her life were recalled and which she could rapidly relate to current symptoms. Her general awareness had improved so much that therapy was concluded. In total some ten hours had been spent in therapy.

In the next Chapter an illustration of the *Free Association* technique will be shown.

*   *   *

CHAPTER 4

"This ... opened my eyes to the fact that it was not necessary to use a dream as the point of departure for the process of "free association" if one wished to discover the complexes of a patient. It showed me that one can reach the centre directly from any point of the compass ..."

- Carl G Jung "Approaching the Unconscious" (from "Man and His Symbols").

We have now looked at *Implosive Therapy* and *Hypnosis,* two techniques used in psychotherapy. Perhaps one of the better-known techniques used and certainly one that I used a great deal in my Practice, however, is *Free Association.* Freud abandoned hypnosis in its favour, calling it *freier Einfall,* or 'sudden idea', which is not quite the same as 'association' but due to Brill's mistranslation has nevertheless become the accepted term in English. The concept refers to ideas that occur *spontaneously* to the client whilst undergoing therapy. When giving a technical definition, Charles Rycroft in *A Critical Dictionary of Psychoanalysis,* explains: "... *Free Association* describes the mode of thinking encouraged in the patient by the analyst's injunction that he should obey the *basic rule;* that is, that he should report his thoughts *without reservation* and that he should make no attempt to concentrate while doing so".

The use of the technique relies upon three fundamental tenets:

1. *Concentration* maximises *resistance* [1], whereas *relaxation* minimises it.

2. All lines of thought tend to lead to what is significant; and

3. the client's therapeutic needs, coupled with the knowledge that he is in treatment, will lead his associations towards what is significant except in so far as *resistance* operates.

As we saw in the first Chapter, the client's problem is stimulated by any sensorial action (touch, smell, taste, sight or sound) associated with it; it follows, therefore, that the very *act of seeking therapy* itself must be stimulating it. That act of making an appointment with the therapist, the subsequent undertaking of the journey to the therapist's practice and verbalising the *effects* of the problem to the therapist, all serve to stimulate it. In this respect the problem is stirred within the unconscious, *waiting* to be released.

1) *resistance* is the technical term for the opposition encountered during treatment to the process of making *unconscious* processes *conscious.* It is a manifestation of *defence.* Resistance manifests itself during free association psychotherapy sessions by failure in the client's capacity to associate freely. It may indeed be necessary on occasions for the therapist to 'switch' from the use of the free association technique to hypnosis depending upon the strength of the resistance he encounters.

The *free association* technique can achieve the ultimate resolution of the chain of associated actions, since it is itself the *most recent* incident on that chain, provided that:-

1. the client is able to achieve a degree of relaxation;

2. reports honestly all thoughts coming into the conscious area of his mind;

3. the therapist is alert enough to identify *repression* and

4. empathy between the client and therapist is achieved at the outset *and maintained.*

Throughout therapy, the problem is brought closer and closer to the conscious mind of both the client and the therapist. Both are unconscious of the underlying problem at the outset except to know and agree that it exists. The proof of its existence is the presenting symptomology of the client, which is not the problem but the client's unresolved method of dealing with it.

It will be evident from what I have said above that sessions will not only involve the free associations of the client but also his *reflections* upon them. His scanning of incidents, which have occurred then, are reported to the therapist. Thus, every association is followed by a period of reflection and discussion. The more experienced the therapist, the better therapy progresses as the client is oscillating "between being the *subject* and *object* of his experience; at one moment letting thoughts come, the next moment inspecting them". According to Sterbs "... treatment requires (the client) to split his ego, one part identifying with the (therapist) and observing and reflecting on the FREE ASSOCIATIONS. In this sense, *splitting* ... is a manifestation of self-awareness ..."

I make no apologies for the length of the following case history; it originally formed part of my Third Report, submitted to the British Medical Association in May, 1988, to illustrate the *Free Association technique* and although in itself lengthy, it probably illustrates the effectiveness of the technique better than pages of explanation could do.

Case History R.176

This client, whom I shall call Arnold, was a teacher of 47 years of age, married with no children. A local doctor referred him to me.

Presenting symptomology: Anxiety state, tension in neck and shoulders. Morbid fear of illness and death. He had suffered glandular fever a few months earlier and had not been able to return to work.

At the initial consultation tests were carried out as a result of which it was clear that Arnold was not suffering any minimal brain damage, also his stress-rating score was low. However, there was evidence of an unfulfilled ambition and a fear of 'unconsciousness'. The possible use of light hypnosis was discussed but Arnold did not like the idea although I explained to him that it might not prove necessary to use a deepening technique.

The *Free Association technique* was eventually used. He drifted back to age 11. It appeared that he was leaning back in a chair when another boy put a foot under it and tipped it right over, causing Arnold to fall back hitting his head on a radiator. He relived the incident well and then drifted to an incident when he was 18 where he was involved in a car accident, injuring the front right hand side of his head, being knocked unconscious and suffering concussion for 4 -5 days. During these 4 - 5 days he told me that he had experienced a peculiar feeling of "remoteness". When asked what fears he had at the time, he answered: "A fear of dependency". He was encouraged to relax and recall incidents of such fears. He then drifted to 10 years of age, to the time when his father had enlisted in the Royal Air Force. He said that he was fond of his father but saw little of him after his enlistment until the war ended and by then his father and his mother were divorced. Arnold then began talking about his brother, three years younger than himself. He said that after his brother was born his parents had engaged the services of a Nanny but he always considered that she was there to look after his brother and he, Arnold, had his mother! At the peak of the Battle of Britain, Arnold was sent to boarding school. He said that he was upset about leaving his mother but relieved that he was away from the senseless bombing. He recalled winning a silver cup for outstanding academic work when he was ten. The episode embarrassed him and afterwards his fears that he would be bullied by other boys proved to be well founded. He recalled an incident where he was held under water by three of the boys and nearly drowned. Other incidents of bullying were recalled too. He confided these incidents to his younger brother, who subsequently told them to his mother. His mother lodged a complaint with the headmaster of the boarding school who then remonstrated with Arnold for telling his mother instead of the teachers and even threatened him with the cane as a punishment for any future conduct like it! He then drifted to age 22 when he had an operation for the removal of his appendix. He said that he recollected the "deep unconsciousness" and a feeling of joy that he was alive when he came round from the anaesthetic. He confessed that since then he had had a fear of being unconscious and had refused anaesthetics. The first session was then terminated and an appointment made for the following week.

At the second session Arnold said that he had enjoyed the first session and had, in fact, returned to work. Unfortunately, there had been a stormy staff meeting and an accident where one of the pupils had fallen from the window of an upstairs room and had been rushed off to hospital. As both these incidents were obviously troubling him, he was encouraged to talk about them. It appeared that the incident with the pupil had stimulated an earlier incident where a pupil he knew had committed suicide. Arnold felt some guilt about this incident because the pupil was something of a friend and Arnold felt that the boy might not have committed suicide if he, Arnold, had been able to get along to talk to him but he was prevented from doing so by illness. This led into the feelings of "remoteness" which he had experienced during the time he had glandular fever and afterwards. He was asked to locate similar feelings whereupon he drifted to age 15 when he was with other pupils in the school Chapel. He said that he felt intense claustrophobia, a feeling of being completely enclosed and pressed in. It appeared that he had nearly fainted and had been helped out of the building. He then drifted back to age 13 when he was standing up in classroom having been called upon to recite a poem from *Pulgrave's Golden Treasury*. He said that he felt peculiar half way through the recitation and fainted — he thought it was something in the poem itself that had disturbed him so. The poem was by William Wordsworth and the point at which Arnold had blacked out was: "We laid waste our powers". He related that his method of learning poetry was to read it through by torchlight under the bedclothes in the dormitory when all the other boys were asleep then afterwards he would go to sleep. In the morning he was able to recall the poem and recite it. Asked why this had affected him he said that he was feeling faint and put his hand to his head. After some moments of silence he said that it was due to masturbation. Just before the incident several boys, including Arnold, had been called into the Headmaster's study and given a lecture on the evils of masturbation by a very embarrassed Headmaster. The therapy session was ended at this point.

At the next session he went back to the incident when he was 11 and his chair had been tipped up. He recalled crashing his head on the radiator and putting his hand to his head and bringing it in front of his face to see it covered in blood.

The following is a verbatim report of the rest of the session. For clarity I have placed my questions to Arnold in bold italics and Arnold's replies in standard type.

"Did the blood upset you?"

"No!"

"What did?"

"That I had hurt my head".

"Why?"

"Because my head is more *me* than anywhere else. I feel panicky. Perhaps I have damaged my brain. The masters and the boys are all crowding round me. I wish that I could be left alone".

(Silence)

"What's happening now?"

"Two of them have picked me up and sat me in a chair. One of the masters is saying 'Tut-Tut!' I expect that's because the lesson has been interrupted. I am now being helped along to the sick-bay and a nurse is cleaning up my head".

"The first time you have ever been attended by a nurse?"

"Yes".

"But have you had cuts before?"

"Oh, yes".

"Who treated you then?"

"My mother".

"Do you wish that your mother is treating you instead of the nurse?"

"No".

"Why?"

"The nurse is kind but *quiet* and doesn't fuss".

"Does your mother fuss, then?"

"Yes!"

"How?

"She overwhelms me! I feel helpless!"

"Tell me about feelings of helplessness".

Arnold drifted back to an incident about a month or two before the chair incident, where there was an air battle overhead between English and German fighter planes. One of the Messerschmidts was hit and the pilot bailed out. The other planes were still machine-gunning.

"What are you feeling?"

"Awful! The German is so helpless, there is nothing he can do".

He drifted to another incident where his mother, his aunt and his cousins were in his aunt's car and nine Messerschmidts came over; his aunt drove the car into the shelter of a barn.

"What's happening?"

"It's silly". (He laughs).

"What is?"

"It has nothing really to do with what I was about to say".

"Tell it anyway!"

"I had just got a new gramophone record and someone sat on it and broke it. Not very important, of course".

"But how are you feeling about it?"

"Most annoyed because there is nothing I can do about it".

"What's happening now?"

"My aunt is driving the car away from the shelter of the barn".

"Have all the German planes gone?"

"We thought they had but a damaged Messerschmidt is flying just above us and it has just started machine-gunning us. My aunt has stopped the car and is saying to us: 'Get out quick!'

We are all piling into a ditch. Machine gun bullets are tearing at the hedge and are hitting the road. The ditch feels damp."

"How do you feel?"

"Helpless".

He then recalled that the German plane crash-landed in a field a short distance away and his aunt ordered everyone back into the car and they belted away like mad from the place.

"Tell me more about helplessness".

"I am 18 years of age and travelling in my grandfather's car. My mother is sitting in front next to my grandfather. I am sitting in the back on the left hand side behind my mother. Next to me is my cousin and next to her, her fiancé. It is my cousin's twenty-first birthday and my grandfather has thought it a good idea to take a breath of sea air at Brighton before taking us all to her birthday party. Oh!"

"What is happening?"

"There is an almighty crash. The car is turning over in the air. Ouch! I have banged my head against the grey-felt roof. I am blacking out!"

"Move on through time a few moments. What is happening?"

"I am laying on my back in someone's garden. I can see green grass, some trees and a bush. My mother is sitting nearby. She is asking me, no *telling* me, that I am all right! What a ridiculous thing to say — I feel anything but all right — really disorientated in fact. There are two St. John Ambulance men peering at me. One of them is saying: 'You're going to hospital'. I am telling them that I am *not*."

"Why?"

"I do not like hospitals".

"Have you been to hospital before?"

"Yes. But never *in* hospital".

"What do you mean?"

"My cousin, John who is 7 is in hospital. I am 11. We had been out together. John felt sick and was ill. He had appendicitis. I am visiting him in the ward but I shall have to get outside as I am feeling sick".

"What is making you feel sick?"

"It's the smell. A horrible smell — ether".

"If you have never been in hospital yourself, why is this smell upsetting you so?"

There was a long silence while Arnold drifted back through the years.

"Ah! I am 6 and in London. A doctor, dentist and a nurse have come to our house. I am in bed and my mother is telling me that I am going to have some teeth out. She didn't tell me what it was like 'though".

"What is it like?"

"Horrible! There is a mask with a tube and they are putting the mask over my face. I can smell it".

"What are you doing?"

"I am trying to push it away but someone is holding my arm down. Oh, dear! It is a terrifying ordeal. I am blacking out!"

"Move on through time a bit.

"I am conscious. I am looking up at a light on the ceiling; it's unlit. I am feeling very sick. I am being sick, really violently sick. Now my brother's Nanny is clearing it up. She has swept-back black hair tied in a bun at the back. She has a longish face, reddish. I feel suddenly very tired. A feeling of remoteness".

"Move on in time to where you are waking up after your sleep".

"Nanny has gone. I am aware of pain in both sides of my lower jaw".

This incident was run out several times until the pain in his lower jaw lifted!

At the following session Arnold said that he was feeling very much better in himself. He remarked that the therapy had been very effective in relieving much emotional stress.

This session he drifted back to age 3. He was living in Richmond and was looking out of the window, which overlooked the river. He saw a barge on fire and one of the boatmen had the back of his coat alight. He related that the man had leaped into the water. Arnold said that the incident had terrified him. When asked to explain his feelings he said that he felt *he* was the boatman. Shortly after this incident Arnold's mother was taken into a nursing home to have a baby.

"Who is looking after you?"

"A woman who is very bossy".

"What does she look like?"

"She looks very much like my mother".

He proceeded to describe being introduced to his young baby brother, who had a lot of black hair. He said that he did not want to get near him.

"Why?"

"I don't like him. I am feeling very jealous. He is crying now".

"What is happening to you?"

"I hate him. I feel like smashing him".

He drifted to several incidents where he was playing with wool toys, which he personalised, thrashing them as if each were his brother. He recalled looking out of his bedroom window at the stars and thinking about eternity, which overwhelmed him. He recalled that his father was kind and that he liked him immensely because he spoke softly and treated him as an equal. Not like his mother who was domineering, commanding.

He drifted back to the incident of the boat on fire and the man jumping into the water. He was obviously reliving something extremely distressful to him.

"What is happening?"

"It is very frightening".

"The fire?"

"No. I think it is *red.* I see him as *red,* jumping into the water. It is the water closing over him that makes me feel so upset".

"Why?"

"I think I must be in a bath. I am sliding to one side and I can't hold on to anything. (Whilst he was talking, Arnold was actually going through some violent movements). I am feeling very frightened. Ah! I am being lifted up; someone is lifting me up".

"What do you see?"

"A colour — white. Now it seems red. It *is* red. I can't see now, it is going black and there is something round my waist"

The next ten minutes or so, Arnold went through birth. That is, he relived his own birth.

Further sessions with Arnold produced his drifting back to the times when he had formulated two main ambitions in life—the first, to be a Barrister; and the second to be a Writer. He had also fancied being involved in politics. It appeared that his involvement in the law had been fulfilled to some extent by his serving as a magistrate for seven years but subsequently from which he resigned because of an inner conflict — he felt that the people up before him on trial had histories which led up to their misdemeanours and that the system paid insufficient attention to this aspect. So far as writing was concerned, he had had articles published but could not devote the time to writing any major works and had accepted the situation. The political ambition had been partially fulfilled by his association with the political party of his choice and helping them at local by-elections and council elections.

He held quite a strong view on capital punishment and was encouraged to talk about this as there seemed to be a lot of emotion involved. It appeared that when he was a young man in Croydon he had been very upset about the Bentley and Craig case. He said that Bentley was an unintelligent man and had been sentenced to death for the murder of a policeman although it was established that it had been Craig, aged 16, who had fired the shot that killed the policeman. Bentley had been unarmed but was adult in years, if not in mentality. Arnold had actually met Bentley's father, mother and sister and also Craig's mother. He had worked hard to get a petition signed for a reprieve for Bentley and was still collecting signatures in the early hours of the morning in which Bentley was hanged. The *utter helplessness* of Bentley and the awful execution had left a lasting impression on Arnold. He was very relieved to be able to release his thoughts and feelings about the incident.

In all, twelve and a half hours were spent in session with Arnold and as his anxiety state had lifted, the tension in his neck and shoulders had gone and he was no longer holding morbid thoughts of illness and death, therapy was concluded. Reports had been sent to his doctor on the result of each session and his doctor had assessed the improvement that had taken place in his patient. The final letter from the doctor is a testimony to the effectiveness of the *free association technique;* it reads as follows:-

"Thank you for all you have done. The improvement in this patient is quite remarkable. Prior to his being referred to you he had been referred to a psychiatrist and had attended for three consultations, which had affected no improvement. The psychiatrist had prescribed stelazine which had produced severe nausea and resulted in (Arnold) terminating psychiatric treatment which he felt was not helping him at all.

I am referring three more patients to you this week who may well benefit from therapy!"

In the next Chapter we will look at Robert Desoille's Directed Daydream technique.

* * *

CHAPTER 5

Narnia Revisited

We are living in the shadowlands
On the dark side of the glass,
And that which seems the end is but
The door through which we pass.
And all the glories of this earth
Are but the stuff of dreams,
Like clouds across the sky through which
A shaft of sunlight gleams.
Within the heart of every child
Of the family of man
Is a subtle spark of memory
Of where it all began.
We are pilgrims on this planet
Cast adrift upon the foam.
We are children of the Universe -
We are waiting to go home.

We have now looked at *Implosive Therapy, Hypnosis* and *Free Association*, which are all techniques of psychotherapy. It will be clear that whatever method of psychotherapy is used, however, some technique has to be employed by the therapist to bring out *abreaction,* the discharge of repressed emotion. It is usually not enough for the client merely to recall an incident in his past, which is affecting him *now;* he needs to release the encysted emotion connected with it.

The *racial memory* is no exception except that its influences are usually more difficult to reach. The most effective method of doing so, in my experience, has been with Robert Desoille's *Directed Daydream.* Racial memories are lurking in the deeper recesses of our being and like the oozing mud of hot springs, send bubbles up to the surface from time to time. This racial memory area is largely one of *fear;* originally fed by rational fears. For example, in Man's earlier history the darkness held much genuine cause for concern as predators lurked there; nocturnal predators whose eyesight was probably far superior to man's. With the discovery of *fire*, however, man was able to shift the balance more in his favour but long after the predators have gone, the *energy* of the fear-memory remains. We can say that the original *cause* has gone but the *effect* remains. Since imagination originally fed those initial fears, led man to accept that there was some survival value attached to them, then is it not reasonable to use imagination to reach and eradicate the problem? In this way, much as in the fundamental principle of Homoeopathic Medicine, we are treating *like* with *like.*

Robert Desoille, a practising Psychoanalyst and Psychotherapist, researched into the method before the second world war, publishing his first description of it in 1938 in *Exploration de l'affectivité subconsciente par la méthode du rêve éveillé.* After the war, his second book, *Le rêve éveillé en psychothérapie* was published in 1945 to be followed by *Psychanalyse et rêve éveillé dirigé* in 1950, *Introduction à une psychthérapie rationnelle* in 1955 and *Théorie et pratique du rêve éveillé dirigé* in 1961. Later, Desoille was to give a series of lectures that were subsequently published in the Bulletin of La Société de Recherché Psychothérpiques de Langue Française. We owe to Frank Haronian, Ph.D. the translation of Desoille's method into English and to the Psychosynthesis Research Foundation, for its subsequent publication in 1966.

I was introduced to Desoille's work that year by my friend and 'Godfather', Roland Northover, with whom some readers may, perhaps, be familiar through his poems which have appeared regularly in both the *Beacon* and *The Seeker* or from his books, *Ask Me Another, Antidote to Fear* and *Out of Chaos,* the last two being co-written with H K Challoner and excerpts from which have also been published in the *Beacon* and *The Seeker*. However, much to my regret, I did not incorporate the Directed Daydream seriously into my Practice as a workable technique until some years later. Roland had spoken frequently and most enthusiastically of the Psychosynthesis Research Foundation, of which he was a member, and also of an approach to both psychoanalysis and psychotherapy which he called *Psychosynthesis,* developed by Roberto Assagioli, an Italian Psychiatrist. Assagioli, a student of Freud and a contemporary of Jung, had pioneered psychoanalysis in Italy. Assagioli was aware of its limitations, however, since neither psychiatry nor psychoanalysis encompassed or embraced what he described as "the higher aspects of man". In those days, although I held Psychoanalysis, Freud, Adler, Jung and many others in high regard, along with the techniques of hypnosis and free association used in psychotherapy, I paid but scant attention to what Roland told me about Assagioli. In fact, it was not until Christmas 1974, when relaxing after my Christmas dinner, that I read in *Psychology Today,* a magazine to which I subscribed, of an interview with Assagioli in which he elaborated on the difference between his view of man and Freud's:

"In one of his letters Freud said - I am interested only in the basement of human being —Psychosynthesis is interested in the whole building. We try to build an elevator, which will allow a person access to every level of his personality. After all, a building with only a basement is very limited, we want to open up the terraces where you can sunbathe or look at the stars. That means that psychosynthesis is holistic, global and inclusive."

It seemed as if suddenly the missing piece of the jigsaw had fallen in place. It had been there all the time, of course, but when involved in the day to day running of a practice, there are very few moments when the therapist has time to reflect upon anything other than the progress of his clients. Christmas provided that break from the practice where there was time to relax and take an overview of things. I had been aware for a very long time that the methods or techniques which I had been employing, effective as they were in reaching certain levels of being and thus capable of effecting improvements, often quite dramatic ones at that, had on occasions, left me feeling dissatisfied. Obviously man not infrequently suffered disharmonious conditions on a *physical* level and a *mental* level for I was fully aware that the body and the mind could interact, for example, as demonstrated in psychosomatic illnesses[1]. Nevertheless, I recognised that man is a complex being who is much, much more than a mobile mass of flesh, blood, bone, hair, muscle and tissue; and even man's possession of a computer called a brain of far greater complexity than that of the animal world was not in itself able to account for phenomena which I had witnessed with many of my clients over the years who, under hypnosis, had regressed not only to incidents in their past but also to what appeared to be distinct recalls of *former lives* which seemed to prove *reincarnation* to be a distinct possibility. With this concept, there was the implication that if we do reincarnate there has to be a *reason* for reincarnating and that line of thought led me to the conclusion that man's consciousness is in a process of *evolution.*

Whenever Roland or Chally were engaged in writing their articles or books they tended to use their friends as "sounding-boards", that is, they threw out their ideas and waited for feed-back. I was no exception to their idea-bouncing games! Naturally, this sort of thing becomes a two-way business of "throw and catch" and can be very stimulating to its participants. I am grateful to those sessions, which helped me enormously and probably still provide valuable thought channels even now. It was during one of our sessions together that we discussed *integrated* man. We concluded that any attempt at healing which denied the existence of the soul, our spiritual being, was incomplete because it provided but two sides of the triangle or encompassed "only one angle" as Roland so neatly put it. Yet many people, including some members of the healing professions, held this limited, one-angled view of man. It is true that some allow that the brain is a collection of cells, many of which "think" or are activated by the input from our five physical senses. The existence of an area governing our so-called 'automatic functions' such as breathing, metabolism, heartbeat, repair and elimination of waste material, is then called for; an unconscious control area of the brain about which little as yet is known. If the brain were merely a computer operating through the physical senses, who or what programmed it in the first place? How does it manage to react to emotion from *within* which can affect not only the five physical senses but its own functioning? As Pascal put it, if we can accept only that which becomes evident through our five physical senses, under which of these five senses does *imagination* fall? Again, when we say that God either exists in *fact* or only in man's *imagination,* we have to define imagination by the use of any one, or a combination of all five, of the physical senses.

A fully *integrated* man is a being endowed with vibrations of a frequency capable of uplifting the physical and mental functioning to a high level, where the vision is expanded to such a degree that Universal or Cosmic Consciousness is

[1] **Psychosomatic**: *Illnesses and symptoms are designated 'psychosomatic' if (a) the symptoms are accompanied by demonstrable physiological disturbances of function, and (b) the symptoms of the illness as a whole can be interpreted as a manifestation of the client's personality, conflicts, life-history, etc.*

attained. Integration enables us to reconcile the unlimited power of the Spirit with the denser vibrations of matter, creating through mental energy, *form*. The variety of form is at once seen to be as limitless as the resources from which it is shaped. Any limitations are seen to be wilfully imposed; that is, we recognise that limits are both unnatural and unnecessary; they belong to the finite realm of the *disintegrated* man. All of us are capable of integration and every one of us will attain it either in this life or in another. Prophets through the ages have tried to point the way out of the treadmill in which we have become trapped, scattering the seeds of truth, hoping that the seeds will eventually take root in the dark occluded minds of man. In their wisdom they saw that to attempt any more than this would have created the *form* upon which disintegrated man would have seized and worshipped; the process of degrading the *ideal* into the *idol* as someone once described it. We are the soil in which the seeds grow or wither. Integration provides the correct balance of *moisture, light* and *air,* which enables the *form* to grow; it does not dictate the form in which they will appear, however. This is freedom in expression; realised *through* integration. The important thing is *that it can be achieved.*

This is what true healing or 'wholing' is all about; to heal is to make whole, the wholing or holy process of integration. Inasmuch as psychotherapeutics are pointed in this direction, they are providing the greatest possible service to those among whom they work. As Roberto Assagioli explains in *Self-Realisation and Psychological Disturbances:*

"The study of the psychopathological aspects of human nature has contributed a vast mass of observations, theories and techniques for the diagnosis and treatment of psychiatric disorders. It has produced the widespread psychoanalytic movement and other aspects of dynamic psychology which have greatly enlarged and deepened our knowledge of the human psyche".

He points out that besides this positive manifestation, however, there is a negative spin-off and that is the unfortunate tendency to place emphasis on the *morbid* manifestations and the *lower aspects* of human nature resulting in the unwarranted generalised application of the many findings to the psychology of normal human beings which has produced a rather dreary and pessimistic picture of human nature and the tendency to depress its higher values and achievements to being derived only from the lower drives, through processes of reaction formation, transformation and sublimation. An approach which ignores many important realities and functions such as intuition, creativity, the will and the very core of the human psyche, the *Self* of which the personal, conscious self or "I" is but a reflection or its projection in the field of personality.

Using the term employed by Goldstein (1939) and Maslow (1954) describing those who are integrated as "self-actualising" individuals he states "... an individual may have genuine spiritual experiences without being at all integrated..." which, of course, is obvious since, in the extreme, to live purely for spiritual experiences with disregard for other aspects of being, is an *imbalance* and not an *integration* of Mind, body and Soul (Self).

What are the obstacles then to becoming an integrated or self-actualising being? Are they nothing more than the *conditioning* influences of our accumulated life experiences? Conditioning may be conscious or unconscious; in either event its effect is to impose limitations upon us. Habit can be said to be a self-imposed condition where a number of thoughts or actions are performed in certain sequence. Repetition has a self-hypnotic effect and diminishes awareness. In the extreme it may produce hallucinations where a part of us attempts to liberate thoughts encysted in the mind into a more creative and stimulating form of expression. If we were to liken *original* thought emanating from Self to pure, unpolluted fresh air and *conditioned* thoughts to various forms of pollution, then we might have a better idea of what is taking place in Man's thoughts and reactions. In such an analogy the fresh air, pure thought, has to pass through the polluted gases, conditioned thoughts, and in the process can become itself polluted to a lesser or greater degree according to the density of the polluted atmosphere around it. When the gases are really dense then the whole thinking process can be out of balance so that a person may appear to be dense or stupid, slow in reaction. Since habit-conditioning may be built up over a long period of time, it is evident that we cannot free ourselves from its effects overnight. Admittedly, there have been some isolated instances where, we are told, there has been a sudden release, a miracle, where the "veil of habit-conditioning has been split asunder", as it were, but accounts of such incidents are somewhat sketchy and whether the released person goes on to live permanently in a higher awareness, self-actualising state, we do not really know.

Moving from the miracle to the more mundane, however, just *how* the habit conditioning can trap us is illustrated by the following:

A man, a business executive, whom I shall refer to as John, sought hypnosis to help him overcome a condition of constipation. Normally he had performed a regular bowel movement every morning shortly after eating his breakfast. One could say that two natural functions were linked; he in-flowed and out-flowed! However, immediately John finished breakfast, he lit his first cigarette of the day, which he proceeded to smoke whilst sitting on the toilet seat. Some days prior to the onset of constipation John had given up smoking. In other words, in this case the *habit-pattern* went something like this: *eating breakfast, the first food of the day, followed by smoking a cigarette, the first one of the day, produces a bowel movement.* John's brain-computer had been programmed over many years and had accepted such a conclusion. Eating, by itself, did not produce the bowel movement, oh no, it had to have the unnatural addition of tobacco smoke to work! In this case it seems that our pressurised businessman had first taken up smoking to help him alleviate stress. He recognised too that in the past he had always experienced difficulty in defecation whenever he had been unable to relax properly. When he realised what was happening, understood the illogical programme which conditioning had foisted on him, John experienced no more trouble; the constipation cleared up within a few days without the use of purgatives. We can see how, in this case, there were two interlinked habits; the smoking habit was being overcome suddenly by the *will* while the nicotine craving, a bodily need which had been set up through habit, sought reinforcement from another habit associated with a body function: "if you give up smoking you will also have to give up bowel actions — this might be bad for you so you had best continue smoking so that you are not ill through constipation". The irrational habit-conditioning was virtually saying: *"Smoking = health; non-smoking = ill-health!"* There are many similar illustrations that could be given to prove how habit-conditioning works to our disadvantage, perhaps even more convincing. However, this particular one, will suffice to make the point.

Habit is defined as a *settled* tendency or practice. I would add that a habit is the result of repetition, which obscures the original purpose. The English language is beautifully descriptive because the word *habit* also means "clothe" or "covering" and that is exactly what habits do, they clothe or cover the original purpose. Ritual may have a purpose but too often that purpose has become lost in the labyrinth of repetition through time, giving birth to superstition, (by definition: an irrational fear of the unknown or mysterious, misdirected reverence, a religion or practice or particular opinion based on such tendencies).

What has this to do with Desoille's Daydream? Well, the point I am trying to make is this: if conditioning can take place like this through habit-pattern associations, demonstrating the power of our *conditioned memory* to affect bodily functions without our realising it, is it not feasible that the *deeply etched* pattern of the *racial memory*, a veritable depository of archetypal fears formed and reinforced over thousands of years, may also affect us adversely? The aim of therapy is to remove inhibited thought or habit patterns that a client may have so that he is more aware, aware that is of his potential as an integrated being, can take responsibility for himself, and ideally effect his own cure. The less inhibited the therapist, of course, the more likely is he able to accomplish this aim.

Assagioli explains in *Self-Realisation and Psychological Disturbances* when drawing the distinction between the Higher Self and the conscious self:

"The conscious self is generally not only submerged in the ceaseless flow of psychological contents but seems to disappear altogether when we fall asleep, when we faint, when we are under the effect of an anaesthetic or narcotic, or in state of hypnosis. And when we awake the self mysteriously reappears, we do not know how or whence — a fact, which if closely examined, is truly baffling and disturbing. This leads us to assume that the reappearance of the conscious self or ego is due to the existence of a *permanent* centre, of a true Self situated beyond or "above" it."

He warns that the Higher Self should not be confused in any way with Freud's "super-ego" which is not a real self but, according to Freud's theory, a construction, an artificial product. It is also different from any "phenomenological" conception of the [lower] self or ego.

He explains: "there are various ways by means of which the reality of the Self can be ascertained. There have been many individuals who have achieved ... a conscious realisation of the Self that for them has the same degree of certainty as is experienced by an explorer who has entered a previously unknown region. Such statements can be found in R.M. Bucke's *Cosmic Consciousness, a Study in the Evolution of the Human Mind,* in P.D. Ouspensky's *Tertium Organum,* in Evelyn Underhill's *Mysticism,* and in other books."

He then points out that the awareness of the Self can also be achieved "through the use of certain psychological methods, among which are Jung's "process of individuation", the techniques of Raja Yoga and Desoille's "Rêve éveillé".

Desoille describes the directed daydream technique as being " ... an intermediate hypnoidal state which shades between wakefulness and sleep" and "is essentially a device for tapping the inexhaustible reservoir in which one accumulates anxieties, fears, desires and hopes (which) maintain their determining influence over ongoing behaviour whenever one is coping with the external world".

It is an ingenious and effective technique. It is, from the mystical viewpoint I believe, a step in attaining the goal of *integration,* the union and blending of the outer and inner, the *alchemical* wedding.

As I mentioned earlier, a client's *dreams*, directed or otherwise, can be of great value to the therapist, aiding psychoanalysis and the subsequent direction of the course therapy may take. All of us dream during the process known as sleep, whether we recall what we have dreamt is another matter. Lewin, in his later papers, distinguished between *screen* dreams (that is, pictorial dreams) and *blank* dreams; the latter being a dream characterised by two convictions on the part of the dreamer: (a) that he has had a dream, and (b) that the dream has no visual content

Charles Rycroft, in his *A Critical Dictionary of Psychoanalysis***,** says this of sleep and dreams**:**

"Although Freud's own writings take sleep for granted, merely assuming that there is a physiological need for it and that the function of DREAMS is to prevent *unconscious, repressed*[(2)], tendencies from disturbing it, the work of Lewin and others suggests that it may itself have a *psychopathology*[(3)] deriving from an unconscious equation of sleep with fusion with the breast (primary identification with the mother). As a result of this equation, excessive sleeping may be manifestation of *regression*[(4)] to the oral level and insomnia may be due either to *ambivalence*[(5)] towards the *internal* (archetypal) mother and dread of fusing with her (it), or, as in *mania,* to the presence of a *phantasy* of being fused with the mother which renders sleep (psychologically) superfluous.

Footnotes:

[1] ***Psychosomatic: Illnesses and symptoms are designated 'psychosomatic' if (a) the symptoms are accompanied by demonstrable physiological disturbances of function, and (b) the symptoms of the illness as a whole can be interpreted as a manifestation of the client's personality, conflicts, life-***

history, etc.

[2] *Repressed: The process of repression is a defence mechanism by which an unacceptable* impulse *or idea is rendered* unconscious. *Freud distinguished between* primary repression, *by which the initial emergence of an instinctual impulse is prevented, and* secondary repression, *by which derivatives and disguised manifestations of the impulse are kept unconscious. 'The return of the repressed' consists in the* involuntary irruption *into consciousness of unacceptable derivatives of the primary impulse, not the dissolution of the primary repression. Repression differs from* inhibition *in that it presupposes the opposition of two* QUANTA of ENERGY; *that invested in the repressed impulse and striving for release, and that invested in the repressing agency* (the COUNTER-CATHEXIS) *striving to maintain the repression, i.e. repression resembles a dam holding back the flow of a river, whereas inhibition resembles switching off an electric light.*

{3} *Psychopathology:* Either *(a) the study of abnormal mental functioning,* OR *(b)* the *theoretical formulation of the abnormal workings of some particular person's mind. Often used loosely to include Psychodynamics, the study of mental processes from a* DYNAMIC *point of view, OR the theoretical formulation of the workings (dynamics) of some specific person's mind, without implying that the processes are abnormal.*

[4] *Regression: In general, reversion to an earlier state or mode of functioning. Specifically, defensive process by which a person avoids, or seeks to avoid,* anxiety *by partial or total return to an earlier stage of* libidinal *and* ego *development. It is not a viable or efficient defensive process since regression compels the individual to re-experience anxiety appropriate to the stage to which he has regressed.*

The term, 'regression' is also used in a rather specialised sense in the theory of dreams *to provide an explanation of the fact that they are hallucinatory phenomena. The theory states that the* Energy *which in waking life would go to the musculature and be discharged in action, is compelled by the* inhibitions *operative in* sleep *to 'regress' to the sense-organs, provoking* hallucinations. The underlying assumption being that the psyche is constructed like a reflex arc with psychic impulses normally moving from the sensory to the motor ends but only in sleep compelled to move in the opposite, regressive , direction.

[5] *Ambivalence: The state of having either or both of two contrary values or qualities. The term was introduced by Eugen Bleuler to describe the co-existence of contradictory* impulses *and* emotions towards the same object. Usually the term refers to the co-existence of LOVE *and* HATE. *Although ambivalence is engendered by all neurotic* conflict *, it is most easily observed in* Obsessional Neurosis, *where an attempt is made to balance the two sides of the ambivalence in* consciousness; *in other neuroses, one or other side is usually repressed*

Recent physiological research has shown that there are two kinds of sleep: normal, or orthodox, and dreaming, or paradoxical; and also that dreaming only occurs in the latter form which can be identified by, *inter alia,* movements of the eye (without opening of the lids) and slow voltage electroencephalic (brain) waves. It also seems likely that the function of dream-sleep is to enable the brain to process the intake of the previous day - the analogy is with a computer, the brain being programmed during the day. If this is correct, Freud's idea that we dream in order to preserve sleep needs reversing - we sleep in order to dream. His theory that infantile tendencies express themselves in dreams is reconcilable with these physiological ideas if one assumes that repressed wishes, phantasies, etc., constitute a backlog of material striving for processing - an assumption which is in line with Freud's own ideas on the role of trauma, traumatic experiences being ones which the subject is incapable of assimilating as they occur. (see Oswald 1966)."

We can now divide *dreams* into one of the following classifications:

1. *Spontaneous Dreams.* That is, dreams experienced by the client during sleep, usually nocturnal, and remembered by him in the waking state. To aid in their recall for subsequent discussion during therapy, I ask the client to keep a notepad and pen on his bedside table to record any significant features of his dreams.
2. *Hypnotically Induced Dreams.* Because dreams can be such a valuable aid in both psychoanalysis and psychotherapy, when hypnosis has been induced a suggestion on the lines of the following can be given: "... you are now in hypnotic time and therefore you can dream for as long as you like but in *actual time* (and that is the time I am in) you are dreaming for sixty seconds. So when I say the word "dream!" you are dreaming for as long as you want in *hypnotic time* but when I say "stop!" your dream (or dreams) will have ended and you are remembering what you have dreamt ..." Although dreams under hypnosis are to some extent imposed upon part of the consciousness of the client, nevertheless there is no *control* of the dream content itself. Free Dreaming is highly valued by me because of its *expressiveness.* In the *waking state* or *awake state*, a client can and sometimes does control what he says in an attempt to defend the *ego;* thus he may attempt to do so in session.
3. *Directed Daydreams.* Unlike spontaneous or normal sleep dreams and those induced through hypnosis, the directed daydream does NOT become a compensatory device because it is *guided.*

For our purposes *all* dreams have:

(a) a *manifest content* that is, the dream as experienced, reported or remembered, and

(b) a *latent content* that is, the dream as interpreted.

The Directed Daydreams are guided in this way:- the client is given a starting image: e.g. a mountain, a seashore, a sword, a chalice and then is asked to describe this image as thoroughly as possible. If necessary, he or she is asked questions to evoke details. The client is reminded frequently during the early work that *in a dream anything is possible.*

Here we come to that special factor which makes for the distinctiveness and effectiveness of the Directed Daydream. The client's imaginary movement in space is *guided by the therapist* and takes place primarily in the *vertical* dimension, either as an *ascent* or as a *descent.* By doing this we are making use of a BASIC LAW OF THE MIND.

To *ascend* may be difficult at first, but ultimately produces images which become increasingly luminous and which express a sense of calm, serenity, and ultimately, joy. What one might term the open and generous feelings, those bright ideas, warmth, lofty thoughts. *Descent* on the other hand, is associated with increasingly sombre images, low deeds, shady deals, the underworld, which may be unpleasant and even quite distressing.

Desoille explains that " ... Among the natural phenomena which affect life, the daily movement of the sun is the most important of all. Sunrise is accompanied by the warmth which assures the well-being and activity of living creatures, and by the light which enlivens the appearance of things and which dispels the pitfalls and the disturbing mysteries of the shadows, so keenly feared by timid creatures. On the other hand, the descent of the sun below the horizon corresponds to the weariness of the day and the depression of spirit, which accompanies the fatigue - as well as to the fears of nocturnal dangers, whether real or imaginary. These impressions, which are renewed for all of us every day with greater or lesser intensity, have put their mark on everyday language..."

There are six standard themes used as starting points, each designed to place the client in a number of symbolic situations, which he must have faced at one time or another in his life. I propose to deal with each of the six themes in turn, providing some examples of their use and will explain their meaning at the conclusion of this book.

First, I ensure that my client is settled *comfortably* in a chair or on a settee. It does not matter whether he or she sits or stretches out in a supine position but it is helpful if the client is isolated from noise and other disturbing distractions. There certainly should be no bright lights, a semi-darkened room is really what is required. When comfortable, I begin by asking my client to take in a deep breath and then, while holding that breath in, to deliberately *tense up* his body from the toes right up to his head and neck, screwing up his face, clenching his jaws, bunching up his fists as tightly as possible and then *holding* that tensed up state for as long as he can ...then, when he feels that he is unable to hold in the breath and all that tension one moment longer, to let that breath out and at the same time release the tension ... and relax. The client is asked to perform this exercise two or three times if necessary until I am satisfied that he has really achieved what I term as being the end product, the reward of genuine effort, a state of real relaxation. Sometimes, instead of the tensing up, followed by relaxing, I have taken my client through what Rosicrucian students of mysticism term the "All-over" or "Over-all" exercise, where the client is asked to concentrate upon all areas of his body in turn, beginning with his feet, then his legs, his waist, etc., right up to his head. This is an exercise that is beneficial in so many ways to a client's well-being; indeed beneficial to the well-being of anyone who performs it.

Daydream 1

Perhaps it goes without saying that it is the *client* who needs to be relaxed, not the therapist! The therapist needs to be very alert throughout for it is incumbent upon him not only to guide his client through the Daydreams but to watch carefully for any signs that the client may be suffering distress.

I usually proceed as follows:

. *"Visualise yourself as being in a meadow, an area of green grass. The sun is shining brightly and you are aware of its warmth on your face. In the distance you see a range of mountains and you begin walking towards them. You have selected one of them, perhaps the one with the highest peak, to climb. Even though you may never have climbed a mountain in your life, remember that anything is possible in a dream.*

"Now, I would like you to begin climbing the mountain. Your object is to reach the peak whatever difficulties you may encounter in the ascent. I want you to describe in detail your ascent of the mountain and what is happening around you. Remember that anything is possible in a dream."

Here is where trouble may begin for although the idea of ascent is relatively easy for some clients who will see themselves doing it quite quickly, to others the climb may demand considerable effort. As Desoille points out: " (for some) the path might be seen as blocked by insuperable obstacles, such as overhanging cliffs, (rocky outcrops), that impede all progress".

It is essential that the therapist should strive constantly to sustain his client's efforts; he must never permit his client to feel abandoned on a note of defeat. On the other hand, it would be quite wrong to insist upon too great an effort, which overtaxes the client's endurance. As soon as there appears to be distress, the client is reminded that in a dream anything is possible and the therapist needs to encourage his client to ensure that he reaches the summit successfully. This may call for considerable effort on the part of the therapist and much ingenuity, for the session must be brought to a close on an affirmative note; in this particular instance, when he has succeeded in leading his client to the top of the mountain. I usually suggest that having reached the summit, the client should rest awhile and enjoy the beauty of the view. I suggest that he might even indulge himself in that deep satisfaction, which arises from having achieved what one has set out to do.

With less inhibited subjects, after again emphasising that in a dream anything is possible, I would continue as follows:

"Above you a few clouds are drifting across the sky and the rays of the sun seem to be piercing the clouds to form a golden stairway. Imagine this pathway formed from shafts of sunlight actually reaching down to the summit of the very mountain where you are.

"Now you are going to do something which requires courage, something which you have never done before but remember that anything is possible in a dream. Step off the mountain peak onto the stairway which seems to be formed of the golden shafts of sunlight and continue your ascent".

It is important, indeed essential, to keep in constant touch with the client's feelings whilst reinforcing his desire to keep climbing.

"As you proceed in your ascent you become aware that someone or something is coming down the staircase from above to meet you. In a dream anything is possible. Your meeting together seems to take place at a natural resting place".

The suggestion that someone is coming from above might provoke varying images. To one person it may be the image of a loved one, to another an elderly character with a white beard, while to yet another, an angelic being. It is interesting, as Desoille points out and which I can confirm from my own experiences, how many clients who might be materialists or "unbelievers" imagine angels.

"Whilst resting there, imagine that you are being given two objects. The first of these is a sword (if the client is a man) **or** *" a vessel or chalice"* (in the case of a woman*). Accept this and examine it closely. Then accept the second object, which is a scroll, rolled up so that you are unable to read what it contains. When you have accepted the scroll, raise your sword or chalice above you as if in salutation and imagine a beam of sunlight striking it; then watch what happens".*

Sometimes modifications occur and are important, for they offer indications of the ease in which a client may adapt himself to the directed daydream technique, whilst also making it possible for the therapist to evaluate the client's capacity for sublimation. All *sublimations* depend on *symbolisation.*

Desoille explains: "One of the important advantages of the directed daydream technique is that it provokes intense emotional reactions very easily". He adds: "This is indispensable for the attainment of certain states of consciousness ..." And so far as effective therapy is concerned, "is essential to the achievement of a cure". It should now be obvious why, in this very first daydream, the therapist must scrupulously avoid anything that might create anxiety.

"Now, imagine that you are being directed to retrace your steps downwards, back to the mountain top where you may rest if you wish or from where you may continue your descent to the base of the mountain.

"You should now examine the scroll whereupon you will discover that it contains an acknowledgement that you have successfully completed the first task which was assigned to you and that there will be five more, the directions of which will appear magically upon the scroll at the appointed time." (Note: In some instances, particularly those where therapy was undertaken more recently, I have suggested that the client should hand back the scroll and accept a scroll in exchange on which his next assignment is given).

At the end of the first daydream, I ask the client to write up *everything* which happened in the ascent of the mountain and beyond and to ensure that the sword or chalice is described fully including any changes which may have taken place in its appearance. If the client experienced any difficulties in the ascent of the mountain and failed to reach the summit, or made the summit but had difficulties in the ascent beyond it, all need to be recorded. This write-up will be brought along to the next session so that its content can be analysed as completely as possible.

Sometimes, of course, another session may be needed to accomplish the whole operation and then, if that fails to produce the desired result, again and again and as many times as is needed until the client is able to make the complete ascent. He is constantly reminded that anything can happen in a dream and occasionally, to ensure a successful conclusion, I have used the suggestion that the client should visualise that someone, or something, for which he has great respect, is responding to his need for help and is giving him support with his task so that he is eventually able to complete it successfully.

* * *

The following illustrations are actual accounts of *Daydream 1* given by clients, selected from several hundred case histories:

Case Ref. G.118

Anna, a waitress, age 44, single, originally consulted me for hypnosis to help her overcome the smoking habit, which proved to be effective and she had ceased smoking altogether. *Later* consulted me again because of stress, insomnia, headaches and morbid hydrophobia, the latter being a condition, she said, which had affected her most of her life.

" I found the ascent of the mountain really tough-going. There were numerous rocky ledges and outcrops with few footholds but eventually I made it to the top. When the golden stairway appeared from the clouds I could not, at first, trust myself to mount the stairs but slowly, one step at a time, I made my way up until I reached the 10th stair. There a white-haired, robed figure appeared whom I identified as *God.* He handed me a chalice, which was of earthenware, brown, plain and shallow. He then handed me a scroll and praised me for my ascent whereupon the chalice changed to a rainbow hue and increased in size and brightness. I descended the stairway and rested in a cave which I found just below the peak of the mountain".

Case Ref. C.133

Barbara, aged 35; married with two sons ages 12 and 11. *Presenting symptomology*: Agoraphobia:

"I began ascending the mountain but managed to get only half way up and didn't feel I could climb the rest. My husband came to help me and he urged me on so that eventually I reached the summit. Here I found 12 steps going upwards into the sky and descending them was a being dressed in black but *faceless.* This being handed me an *urn,* grey-white in colour, large and stony like a cremation urn. I descended the mountain without problems."

Following this session, Barbara recalled her late father's cremation, which had filled her with such disappointment that she pleaded with her mother to have a second service at the local church. (She seemed to have some repressed guilt feelings associated with her suggestion as her mother was upset by the idea).

Case Ref. F.19

Eleanor, age 43, a professional healer, widowed with two grown up children (a daughter, age 25 and a son, age 21) not living at home. She had had several lovers since the death of her husband several years previously but none of these had proved to be satisfactory or lasting. *Presenting symptomology*: intermittent depressions, inability to achieve orgasm with resultant feelings of frustration and anger.

Eleanor had excellent visualisation and described most articulately the scenery. Her mountain was "clad in vegetation where there were birds of infinite variety and a beautiful waterfall. I found a pathway which made the ascent reasonable easy"

She described the higher part of the mountain as "naked" but here "a Merlin-like figure, clothed in a blue-grey cloak and large hat, came to meet me. He had a benevolent, bearded face and hooked nose. We ascended the mountain together. At the top "Merlin" rewarded me with a chalice which was silver with a deep-cut square base and glittering with splendour. He then handed me a scroll explaining that it contained instructions that I was to read at the appointed time but until then I must rest awhile in a cave nearby. I found this most comforting. I held up the chalice in a gesture of salute and noticed that the chalice was overflowing with an inexhaustible effervescence"

Case Ref. G.93

Anita, age 38, married, had been working as a nurse before the birth of her daughter some seven or eight years prior to the onset of the problems about which she had approached me. *Presenting symptomology*: Anxiety state; agoraphobia.

" The sun was shining brightly as I walked across the green grass and climbed the highest mountain in the group. The going was tough at first but I persisted in my ascent and reached the peak. At the top of the mountain there were steps to climb through a cloud where I was met by an Angel - a very kind and peaceful Angel, wearing a long white robe. The Angel gave me a scroll and told me that I had to follow its instructions. I was also given a shiny, white porcelain vessel which I kept in a protective bag around my waist".

Case Ref: L.70

Colin, a young College student, was suffering both anxiety and difficulty in coping with relationships. His studies were affected.

"I found that I was able to climb the mountain to the top although there were many obstacles on the way - loose rocks, sheer, smooth faces of rock where it proved difficult to gain footholds and several times I was attacked by black eagles which I had to fend off with one hand. On reaching the top, I was told that I had to climb still further and proceeded to make my way up a stairway of golden sunlight. I had climbed some thirty stairs when I encountered what I can only describe as *Pure Light* coming towards me. This Light bore with it a sword and a parchment. I sensed that these were being offered to me so I accepted them both. The sword was of the finest gold with an ornate hilt encrusted with jewels..."

Case Ref. M.37

Rita, age 46, single, a SRN, had suffered a severe asthma attack some six months previously during which her heart had stopped beating; she had been resuscitated by a colleague. After this Rita had become very depressed and suffered other symptoms of a distressing nature such as arthritic type pains, stomach upsets, shaking and "restless leg" syndrome.

"The mountain had a blue-grey summit with an eagle circling it. The sides of the mountain were very rocky with grass on the lower slopes and areas of loose shale. I used a rope to enable me to ascend by *lassooing* pointed outcrops and in this way pulled myself up to the next level. Making my way tenuously like this I eventually reached a stream rushing down over rocky protrusions and found it a little easier to climb there. The peak of the mountain, however, was very narrow and pointed. I stood on an outcrop of rock wondering how to ascend the final stage to the peak when one of the eagles came down, alighting nearby and urged me to follow it around the other side of the mountain. I did so and was pleased and surprised to see a grassy slope leading to the very peak. At the peak there was a shaft of golden light around a flight of 144 stairs leading up into the sky. Angels lined this stairway and there were many of them and they were all joyous. An old man came down the stairway - he had a red cape embossed with gold, white hair and a beard. Beneath his cape he had green clothing. He had a crown but this was way behind him. His arms were outstretched, holding a chalice towards me. I accepted the chalice which had a white marble base in which a large sapphire was set. The chalice is of silver-gold with open handles, one on each side. Inside the chalice was a liquid which looked like water but tasted like nectar. The old man also gave me a scroll which contains information about my next assignment. He told me to keep the chalice and bade me either to return to the base of the mountain ready for my next assignment or to remain on the mountaintop to rest and tarry awhile. I elected to remain and when I saluted him with the chalice it took on the appearance of the sun with golden rays streaming from it".

Case Ref: M.164

Sylvia, single, aged 26, a shop manager. Youngest of a family of five. (one brother and three sisters). Presenting symptomology: Obesity, frigidity (Rape victim 2 years previously, the rape being at knife-point by the rapist who was committed to prison having murdered another victim).

"I can see the grass meadow and the mountain but I am unable to get to it; to even approach it! It is like something is holding my feet". These were her words at the time she was in therapy. She was obviously very distressed so after explaining to her that in a dream *anything can happen,* I said that whatever was holding her feet, therefore, had to release sooner or later. Whereupon she managed to cross the meadow. However, after crossing the meadow to the foot of the mountain, she was incapable of scaling it even though she had climbed mountains in real life! Eventually, after a considerable lapse of time and reminders that *in a dream anything can happen*, she ascended by balloon. Having gained the mountaintop in this way she saw clearly the stairway leading up into the sky but was not happy about stepping onto it. After a very long silence she broke it by saying:

"I have stepped onto the first stair but I feel very shaky".

I explained that having taken this first step, which required courage, and bearing in mind that in a dream anything can happen, could she not take the ascent "one step at a time". In this way she slowly climbed a few more steps and was surprised to see a figure of a monk in a habit on the stairs above her.

"The monk is bearded, he looks rather like a picture I once saw in a bible".

When asked to describe the chalice that he handed her, she said: "It is a golden chalice and has figures on it which I cannot make out".

The scroll was "rolled up" like a parchment. She was unable to tell me anything more about the chalice except to say that although it had figures on it - it was empty.

Sylvia descended the mountain on foot with no problems, deciding to wait there to rest before undertaking the next assignment. It was fortunate that this was my last session of the day because it lasted considerably longer than the hour she had booked!

Case Ref: M.130

Carl, age 31, single, occupation: long distance lorry driver. *Presenting symptomology*: feelings of anxiety and stress. Disliked aspects of his work since it provided little opportunity for social life or for forming any lasting relationship with a member of the opposite sex.

Ascended the mountain and stairway from the clouds quite easily. The figure descending to meet him he recognised as being Jesus, the Christ. Asked how he knew that it was Jesus, he replied that he knew *instinctively.* The *first* sword, which Jesus handed to him, was described as being silver and straight but subsequently a *second* sword, with a curved blade and mother-of pearl crooked hilt also appeared in his hand. He said that he felt he was being asked *to make a choice.*

Case Ref: O.45

Michaela, aged 17, factory worker. *Presenting symptomology:* Vomiting either during or after meals, underweight by at least 2 stone, difficulty in responding to her boy friend's affectionate advances; difficulty in keeping up with her quota at work.

She was able to ascend the mountain but not without difficulty and prompting. After initial hesitation she was persuaded to begin ascending the stairway from the clouds.

"A man who looks just like my grandfather is descending the stairway towards me. I always respected my grandfather - he was always so kind and gentle. He is handing me a chalice which has 2 gold handles and is studded with rubies and diamonds ..."

From that point on, her attitude changed, she co-operated well throughout therapy, completing all of the daydreams and eventually made a complete recovery.

Case Ref: S.164

Warren, aged 39, living with his parents since his divorce three years previously. *Presenting symptomology:*

Anxiety, various aches and pains and feelings of exhaustion. Warren had recently met a woman whom he liked very much but the relationship seemed to be causing him some anxiety.

Warren's ascent of the mountain produced a problem by way of a jagged outcrop of rock that he thought was "impassable". He could not describe the outcrop, which resembled a face, so eventually drew it on a sheet of paper. Whilst studying it he realised that it was *his mother's face.*

Case Ref: T.68

Stuart, age 24, single, living with his father. *Presenting symptomology:* Introspective, intermittent bouts of depression.

On ascending the mountain he said that everything seemed as if it was taking place "in slow motion". Eventually he reached the peak and then began the ascent of the stairway into the sky. A figure descended to meet him whom he identified as Jesus. The sword, which he accepted from Jesus, he described as being like Excaliber, strong and shining. He was reluctant to go back down the stairway "because it is too mundane below". He finally did make the descent but confessed that he had had to "force himself down".

Case Ref: W.154

Beryl, age 41, married, employed as a Health Club Receptionist. *Presenting symptomology:* Headaches, panic attacks, depression.

At first, experienced difficulty in ascending the mountain but eventually recognised that she could "do anything in a dream" and *flew* up the mountain. In like manner she tackled the stairway but was unable to ascend very high because of a gaping hole, which appeared in the stairway. The hole was so formidable that she had to return to the mountaintop "to rest and to recover (her) strength" before making another attempt. *It took two psychotherapy sessions* to get her to cross a platform and bridge the hole, where she was confronted by a statue of the Christ. She identified this as representing her inability to reconcile her deeper religious feelings with the dogmas of orthodoxy - "the Christ was a statue, not a Spirit".

After recognising why this had happened she asked to do the Daydream again and this time encountered a living Being, dressed in a white robe, descending towards her with arms outstretched.. She described the chalice he later gave her as being "highly coloured, classically shaped and of Indian brass".

* * * * * * * *

From these illustrations it will be clear that Desoille's observations given below are indeed evident even after but a modest acquaintance with the technique:

1. There is an extreme variety in the detail and content of the responses evoked but this richness of content is presented by a subject within his or her own fairly fixed personality pattern.
2. There is an extraordinary richness of imagery in certain especially talented subjects.
3. There is an apparent shift in the style of the imagery so that it progressively departs from one's memories of reality and from the habitual memory of nocturnal dreams.

In future parts of this book we will be looking at other aspects of the Directed

Daydream with illustrations including one that was written up entirely in verse by the client and confirms classically Desoille's second observation above.

*   *   *

CHAPTER 6

"Just remember, in the winter,
Far beneath the bitter snows
Lies the seed
That with the sun's love
In the spring
Becomes the rose."
- from Bette Midler's "*The Rose*"
*

In the last chapter we examined, in some detail, the first of Desoille's Directed Daydreams and we were able to see just how the use of the technique could bring forth a rich response as each client was encouraged to draw upon his or her imagination. In the final part of this book I will reproduce the most striking example of this, an unique write-up of her experiences given by a young woman who changed her life style entirely after completing all six of the daydreams.

However, let us now look at a definition of *imagination* as given in Charles Rycroft's, *A Critical Dictionary of Psychoanalysis.*

> "IMAGINATION (is) the process, or faculty, of conceiving *representations* of objects, events, etc., not actually present. The process produces results that are either:
> (a) *imaginary,* in the sense of being fictitious, unreal, etc., or
> (b) *imaginative,* in the sense of providing solutions to problems which have never previously been solved or, in the arts, creating artefacts which none the less reflect or enhance experience. The psychoanalytical literature tends to subsume imagination under the heading of PHANTASY and has the same difficulty as do the arts in deciding whether and when phantasy (imagination) is escapist or creative, defensive or adaptive.
> It is generally accepted that creative imaginative activity involves the participation of unconscious non-verbal phantasy".

In the sense that we *all* use imagination, as Rycroft says, to solve problems, there would seem to be a very strong case for the use of Desoille's technique to enable us to solve problems however deep-seated their nature; including those which hitherto had had no way of being solved. The scientist or the inventor will collect and study all *known* data on something he is researching and then will have to use his *imagination* to make that connecting link between *fact* and the successful culmination of his work. Each successful outcome, bridging the gap between what has been known hitherto and what is now known, owes its discovery to imagination. Imagination is the greatest gift that God has bestowed upon man.

Experience in the use of Desoille's Directed Daydream technique led me to introduce one or two refinements of my own. For example, I have found that the six daydreams, instead of being worked through as isolated exploits, are best *linked together.* I have achieved this by introducing the idea of the *scroll.* The scroll is given to the client at the same time as the sword or chalice and contains instructions that appear magically at the very beginning of each "assignment". In this way, the client is able to accept the Daydreams as a *continuing* process. This continuity, after all, is but following the assumption of Freud's "free association" technique: (1) that all *lines of thought* tend to lead to what is *significant,* (2) that the client's therapeutic needs and knowledge that he is in treatment will lead his associations towards what *is* significant (except in so far as *resistance* operates), and (3) that resistance is minimised by relaxation and maximised by concentration.

Resistance manifests itself during sessions by failures in the client's capacity to associate *freely.* The Daydreams in isolation, as originally conceived and used by Desoille, were designed to lower the incidents of resistance and thereby " ... shorten the time of treatment". Desoille admits that "... the resistive attitude is sometimes encountered in a patient during the course of a directed daydream but is much rarer than in psychoanalysis because the patient, expressing himself in pictorial language, exerts much less censorship over his self-exposure which, in a manner of speaking, takes place involuntarily. But in one way or another, the facts finally present themselves". Desoille then gives an illustration from a case history of one of his patients, Jeanne, a woman separated from her husband, by whom she has had two daughters, the elder of whom went to live with her father, whose side she took in the parental dispute, while the second stayed with her mother and is the joy of her life. It appears that when she was seven years of age, Jeanne had been caught in an animal trap and as an unfortunate consequence of that painful event, was separated from her own mother for a period of time. Desoille describes Jeanne as being not only a very intelligent woman but has talent as well. She had previously sought a solution to her problems "in a kind of private asceticism; she had also engaged in the spiritual exercises of several different schools such as Zen, Freudian psychoanalysis, not to mention other lesser known cults". He adds that in her shopping around, she decided that she wanted to try directed daydreams too! During the first directed daydream, *resistance* is encountered which Desoille's describes as follows:-

"At first, all goes well, and I get her to begin climbing a high mountain. Thus, she arrives at a pass next to a field of snow, feeling quite well, she says. I suggest that she rest for a moment, then I invite her to take off again towards the summit. At this point, Jeanne balks and declares: 'I like it here and I don't want to go any farther!' I urge her on and try to get her to try again. Jeanne refuses to do so. She opens her eyes and says: 'No, I'm not interested in that!"

Here is an example of obvious resistance. What motivated it? The short anamnesis, which preceded the directed daydream, provided me with enough information to make a guess. Whenever Jeanne attempts something new and feels that she might get deeply involved in it, the latent memory of the trap in which she had been caught as a child forces her to withdraw in order to avoid the danger of being caught again"

Desoille tells us that he stuck to the daydream approach, for to have done otherwise would have been a betrayal of his deepest convictions. He says that gently but firmly he insisted that Jeanne closed her eyes and then, when she had done so, he encouraged her to re-establish the pleasant image she had previously held, thus finding the calm (relaxation) needed to proceed. After asking her to have the image of her daughter appear beside her, which she did, he asked her to describe the girl's image. Jeanne described her young daughter as "a girl smiling and full of energy". Desoille, using the potential of that image to the full, suggested to Jeanne that her daughter was taking her by the hand and urging her towards the summit, which she wanted to explore. He says that this procedure was completely successful in overcoming Jeanne's resistance and that he was able to bring the session to a normal conclusion. He points out that adherence to a different theoretical explanation can lead us to find new procedures and *shorten the time of treatment.*

In this example, given by Desoille, although he has not said *why* he asked Jeanne to rest for awhile after she reached the pass in her first attempt, I think we can assume that he was observing his client closely while she verbalised her dream, watching for any sign that she might be experiencing difficulties and that he did notice something different in Jeanne's facial or bodily expression as she came to the mountain pass. I believe, from similar experiences with my own clients, that Jeanne became aware of something on her image-screen at that point, which contained sufficient similarities to reactivate the unpleasant, repressed memories of the unfortunate accident she had suffered as a child. Perhaps the animal trap had been hidden in the snow, which is why she had not become aware of it until she had become entrapped in it. Perhaps there were other screen images too which restimulated the memory of that accident, this incident in her life that caused her both physical pain and subsequently the emotional pain of the loss (separation from) her mother. The interesting point about it was that she then attempted to assure Desoille that she was "feeling quite well", that was, of course, untrue but she was not only trying to put him off recognising that there was anything wrong; but at the same time seeking to reassure herself that she was feeling well. I have no doubt that she wanted to avoid being trapped into a situation which she was not ready to face at that point. Desoille identified this classic example of resistance and used his imagination, his ingenuity, to get her to "return to session".

The keynote is that of getting the client to *relax.* The Directed Daydreams, as six isolated experiences, whilst certainly not *maximising* resistance, nevertheless tended to produce *less* relaxation than was the case when they were linked. This proved to be so in a significant number of the clients I treated *(over 85 %).* Basically, the Daydreams were designed to minimise *resistance* since they enable a client to come to terms with the archetypes through six imaginative experiences each taken in isolation. Linking the assignments in the client's mind, as I have said, resulted in a gradual increasing of relaxation as he or she progressed through the daydreams.

I believe that relaxation is achieved through *confidence;* this may be the confidence the client has in the therapist to begin with but as therapy progresses, ideally the client achieves more confidence in himself and becomes more relaxed in consequence. Indeed, it could be said that the achievement of complete relaxation is the ultimate goal and can only be attained when a person has complete confidence in himself.

In the last chapter we referred to a BASIC LAW OF THE MIND which is a special factor in the distinctiveness and effectiveness of the Directed Daydream, the client's imaginary movements being guided by the therapist primarily in the *vertical* dimension, either as an *ascent* or as a *descent.* Whilst the first daydream dealt with the ascent of the mountain and the subsequent ascent beyond the mountain's peak, the second daydream is very much one of a descent, into the depths of the ocean.

Before the client embarks on his second "assignment", he is warned that he is about to be guided to descend into the depths of the ocean and that this will probably stimulate the appearance of unpleasant, possibly horrible, images. However, he is asked to face them bravely since that is the only way to discover the origin and character of one's anxieties and the way it is possible to learn how to conquer them and to dispel them gradually. Desoille says that he immediately offers his clients " the reassurance that this new (second) daydream "... will end with a pleasant scene which will leave (the client) in a comfortable state".

Desoille goes on to say that " ... after these preparatory remarks, I ask the client to imagine a seashore, a rocky coast where the water is very deep. After the client has described this scene, I suggest that he imagine putting on either a diving suit or a scuba outfit and that he let himself slip into the water, descending as deeply as possible. As he does this, I urge him to tell me in detail what he sees in his mind's eye. In general, feelings of fear arise quite quickly ...".

At this point I would like to quote from Anna's account of her second daydream. Readers may recall that Anna was the 44 year old **(Case Ref: G.118)** whose first daydream was shown at the beginning of the illustrations in the last chapter.

" I descended the mountain, not without difficulty but eventually used the chalice to scoop out footholds. About one third of the way down I got stuck and could neither move up nor down. Several minutes must have elapsed until I noticed a tuft of grass to my left, which I grasped and was able to swing across onto a goat's footpath. *(She actually described a goat that was on it).* When I had descended about half way I saw a cave on my right and I was tempted to rest there but I put the temptation aside and decided to carry on down. I was nearly at the bottom when I encountered a sharp ledge and rocky outcrops that were very muddy. A lot of water was coming down from the mountain and I did not like it.

However, I pressed on over it and reached drier land again, where the going was easier but still muddy underfoot. I reached a grassy plateau where I decided to take a brief rest and then kept going. Eventually the slope became very steep, forcing me to run. I slipped over several times but picked myself up and continued until I reached the bottom. I made my way over some grassy meadowland to the top of a cliff overlooking the sea. I peered over hoping to find a way down the cliff to a ledge below and after a lot of searching discovered a path. Its access had been obscured by bushes but as the cliff-top was becoming crumbly I hastened down the pathway to a ledge just above the surface of the sea. There I selected a scuba outfit and put it on. I then descended into the ocean. I saw lots of fish swim past me including some swordfish. Two sharks swam past me. It was very light under the water. I saw a school of barracuda out there but they presented no real danger. Another shark came towards me but then quickly turned away again. I continued to descend — a long way down, much deeper I could tell because it was much darker. Then I saw the ocean bed. Just near was the entrance to a grotto, which looked very eerie, a substance like black tar lined its walls that were about three feet apart. I felt very afraid as it was so dark. I saw something bright red with horny skin —horrible — it was lying down and was quite enormous. Then it moved. It had a massive mouth, razor-sharp teeth like a crocodile's mouth. I did not like it, for although its eyes were closed, its tail was lashing out. To escape the tail, I seemed to move very close to its mouth, about three inches away. Then the head moved. The head had sort of antennae on it. I swam away from it, back to the lashing tail. I decided to swim in closer and touched it with my chalice, which immediately tamed it. Inside the grotto there were old shipwreck pieces. I made my way back to the ledge and discarded the scuba outfit; the monster had followed me. On the ledge were many snakes— black and green — so many of them. One snake knocked the chalice out of my hand and I had to use the scroll to pull the chalice away from it. I gripped the chalice tightly. The monster was sitting on the ledge with me; the snakes had all slithered under the ledge. I thought that my chalice had frightened them away. I touched the monster with the chalice whereupon it turned into a black horse, like Black Beauty. It led me up the cliff path and at the top I mounted it and rode to the foot of the mountain. Together we climbed the mountain, the horse missing its footing only once from which it recovered rapidly. We ascended the golden stairway together and on the ninth stair we met God. He handed me the third scroll as I raised my chalice to Him. The chalice seemed to have changed, being much larger, yellow in colour and very shiny, glazed and smooth. I descended the stairway, and then the mountain, to a cave where I decided to rest before setting out on my next assignment.

One of Anna's problems had been a morbid fear of water, which she had suffered since an infant. Under normal circumstances, therefore, a descent into the water would have been impossible for her but with the use of the Daydream and reminders that "in a dream anything can happen", Anna made the descent to the bottom of the sea. Shortly after the session above, Anna made a decision to change her employment from that of a waitress to what she considered to be a much more worthwhile occupation, that of a nurse. However, in subsequent parts of this article I propose showing Anna's progress and that of the other clients mentioned, as they undertake the Daydream assignments.

Barbara's Second Daydream (Case Ref: C.133):

"I descend into the sea depths and encounter a monster so large that it fills the grotto in which it lives. By using the urn I am able to tame the creature whereupon it turns into "Puff, the magic dragon". I reascend but it follows me so I touch it once again whereupon it becomes a handsome fairy-tale Prince. I reascend the mountain and at the summit I lift the urn to the sun. The urn now turns into a silver trophy-cup on a black stand".

Eleanor's Second Daydream (Case Ref: F.19):

"My rest over, I descended the mountain in the company of an *Owgle* (a cross between an Eagle and an Owl, representing both power and wisdom). I crossed the grassy meadow to the cliff and found a path but there was a gap in it and I was forced to jump this and thereby gained a ledge overlooking the sea, on which there was a diving suit and a light scuba suit. The scroll directed me to choose one or the other of these and then descend into the depths of the ocean. I chose the lighter gear and descended into the depths. A porpoise befriends me *(note the change of tense)* and guides me through the weeds in the waters. Soon I see a grotto guarded by a monster - a huge creature, blackish-green with 12 heads. I am relieved to discover the Owgle has appeared by my side. Together we confront the monster whereupon 11 of its heads are lost and the remaining one is a brighter green and not so fearsome. It is now offering me the contents of the grotto - an old book with faded writing in copperplate, and some pressed flowers -a pansy, a forget-me-not and a clover. I also see a treasure chest which is locked but I am forcing it open with a rusty tube I have found and discover the contents to be fine robes and jewels. The chest becomes smaller when I close the lid and I decide to take it away with me together with the old book. I am now making my way back through the water, which is of a lighter hue; the monster is following me. I touch it whereupon it has turned into a young man in his prime, physically most attractive and standing in a Viking-like boat in full command. I am reluctant to let him go but somehow receive an inner assurance that he will always be there. I make my way back up the cliff and across the meadow. It has become dark and cloudy as I cross to the mountain and begin the ascent. The mountain is bathed in sunlight up to its peak where the Owgle waits. I step onto a golden stairway leading upwards and at the top meet an Angel with male appearance but actually androgynous. I hand the Angel the book and the treasure chest. The Angel congratulates me and hands me the next scroll. The effervescence from my chalice merges with the Angel's own light into a perfect blending. After this I descend to the mountain peak and rest in the cave there with the Owgle".

Anita's Second Daydream. (Case Ref.: G.93):

"The first instruction was to walk back down the steps, down the mountain, across the grass, down a cliff-path to an outcrop of rocks. The sea under the rocks was rough. On the rocks I rejected the heavy diving suit that was there, choosing to wear a lighter, frogman's outfit. I went into the sea, which was light at first, dark later, and down to its bed, passing some small fish and weeds. On the seabed I met a placid monster in human form, at the entrance to its cave. The cave was made of rock and its entrance was very large. The monster was silent and wore a full-length charcoal coloured gown with long sleeves; the head was partly covered but I could just see a mask-like sad face. It is just not really human but just there. In the cave I saw a four-poster bed with no canopy and on the bed, a patchwork quilt worked in mainly reds and pinks. Even if offered, I couldn't take anything from the cave to keep - I don't think there was anything other than the bed and I couldn't take the cover and leave it without. I didn't really want a souvenir of this trip! The scroll directed me to swim back to the surface, taking the monster with me. On reaching the rocks, I touched the monster with my vessel (I had formerly touched it on the sea bed to tame it, although it was quite docile and did not need taming). The monster did not immediately change form but when I persisted in touching it with the vessel it became a teddy bear like Shelley's hand made one. The bear was French-mustard coloured (I couldn't describe the colour before!), solid, rigid limbs with large, round unattractive eyes....."

At this point she exclaimed: *"This is my dad!"* and burst into sobbing. She cognised that the teddy bear was symbolic of her father, both being somewhat sad figures. In fact, the whole of her childhood seemed to be symbolised by the teddy-bear and the stiff unbending attitude of her mother, as a consequence of which she felt that both the bear (her father) and she, herself, had missed out in life.

Later , she was able to proceed with her narrative:

" ... I then made my way back along the cliff path, across the grass, climb the mountain and continue up the steps through the cloud and back to the Angel. I did not take the teddy bear with me. I told the Angel that although I had completed the mission, I had met with problems with a couple of tasks. When I showed the Angel my vessel its appearance was almost the same as when I had left, possibly not so bright. When the sunlight caught it, however, there seemed to be a thin gold rim round the top".

Colin's Second Daydream (Case Ref. : L.70):

"The descent into the deep waters in the light diving gear presented no real difficulty for me. I felt ready to face the monster for I had my sword ready. The monster proved to be an octopus of considerable size. Although it was aware of me it did not attack me because it seemed to know that I held in my hand a weapon capable of destroying it. I touched the octopus with the tip of the sword and this seemed to tame it. I made my way back to the rocks on the shoreline, the octopus following me like a dog. I touched it once again with my sword and it changed into an ordinary looking man. I left it behind me and reascended the mountain without difficulty, ensuring that I climbed in the same approach as before. Once more I stepped onto the stairway of golden sunlight and met the Light. I reported the accomplishment of the second mission and sensed that I had done well. On raising my sword in salutation to the Light it gleamed brightly. I elected to return to the base of the mountain before setting out on my third mission".

Following this daydream, Colin was asked why he thought the monster had changed into an 'ordinary man'. He was hesitant at first and then said that somehow the metamorphosis from octopus to an ordinary man had caused him much concern. He identified the emotion of fear but could not see why. After discussion he agreed that his greatest fear was that of becoming just an *ordinary* man.

Rita's Second Daydream (Case Ref.: M.37):

" I used my cape to fly down the mountain and made my way to the cliff overlooking the sea. I descended the cliff by way of a pathway, which led to a ledge just above the water level. There I selected a scuba diving outfit rather than the heavier diving gear that was also available. I lowered myself into the water, which was very blue with darker green patches caused by seaweed with fronds like ferns. These in no way impeded my progress, however. Bright goldfish swam past me. On the floor of the seabed are many shells. I entered a grotto, which I knew was the home of the monster I had to face. The monster is like an octopus but dark brown in colour. It was not large but had numerous grey-coloured tentacles. It saw me but did nothing. It looked as if it ought to have been doing something but was not. It had nice eyes rather like a spaniel and as I looked at them I realised that it was unhappy! I touched it gently with my chalice whereupon its colour changed to a sand colour. I looked around the grotto: there were electric eels and bells, large ones. Also, a typical pirates' chest containing jewels. There was nothing there in that grotto that I wanted so I made my way back to the ledge. The monster followed me there so I touched it again with my chalice and found that it turned into a fairy prince, godmother and a unicorn - the personality of the unicorn predominating but the other 'presences' were there also. I was aware that although I had taken nothing from the grotto in a physical sense, I did take with me the *sound* of bells. I mounted the unicorn and ascended the mountain with no difficulty. I then ascended the golden stairway. The stairs were lined by angels who were all wearing pale blue gowns. They were all singing beautifully ... like the Hallelujah Chorus. The stairway seemed less steep than before and after I had ascended only 77 stairs it seemed to flatten out. An old man, bent with age and wearing a brown robe, stepped forward to meet me, holding a shepherd's crook in one hand. He had white hair and a white wispy beard. His eyes were very twinkly, giving me the impression that he knew a lot and that his *interior* is greater than the exterior appearance he presented. As he talked to me he straightened up and became very tall. I accepted the third scroll assignment from him and raised my chalice towards him. The appearance of the chalice itself was as before but surrounding it was a light of blue, green and turquoise ... yet there was also purple in the light. The unicorn left my side and went with the old man. I decided to return to the top of the mountain before undertaking my next assignment".

Sylvia's Second Daydream (Case Ref. : M.164):

" ... I had no hesitation in sliding off the ledge and descending into the ocean; in fact I actually enjoyed the experience. I soon found the grotto with the monster — a Godzilla creature".

Asked to describe it she replied: "It's the opposite to King Kong and Kong defeated it".

I asked her: *"Who is Kong?"*

She replied: "Kong was the beast who loved the woman!"

She seemed quite unafraid and, using her chalice, touched Godzilla and tamed it. She then went on a tour of its cave but found nothing of interest to her there. She ascended to the ledge with Godzilla following. She said that she removed the (heavy) diving suit and as Godzilla reappeared she touched him once again with her chalice.

At this point she seemed obviously surprised and exclaimed: "It's turned into Lisa!"

"Who is Lisa?"

"Lisa is my Dalmatian dog. Originally she was Jamie's dog (Jamie is her boy-friend). It is a bitch but aggressive and can tackle other dogs fearlessly".

She reascended the cliff, the mountain and climbed as far as the seventh stair but was held back by Lisa who had difficulty in climbing the stairs and had to be helped. The monk met her there and she accepted the scroll with her third assignment. She described the chalice as shining brightly. She descends the stairs and the mountain without difficulty, deciding to rest at the foot of the mountain before setting out on the third assignment.

Carl's Second Daydream (Case Ref. : M.130)

His descent was one "...into dark waters". His monster " ... an evil, snake-like creature".

He overcomes his fear of it and after a fierce battle eventually manages to get close enough to pierce it with the *first* sword which subdues it. He reascends and climbs onto the ledge to discover that the monster has revived and is climbing onto the ledge too. This time he uses the *second* sword and immediately he touches the monster, he exclaims:

"It has turned into a Mermaid!"

"You seem surprised. What does a mermaid represent to you?"

"A creature half-woman, half fish". (Silence) and after some considerable time: "I wonder *why* it has caused me concern".

Further long silence broken eventually by his exclaiming: " I have had difficulty in forming a lasting relationship with women".

"Has that caused you a lot of worry?"

"Oh! Yes, I thought that I might be thought to be homosexual!"

Michaela's Second Daydream (Case Ref. : O.45):

"I choose the light weight diving suit but when I am told to lower myself into the water I am afraid to do so".

After a lapse of a few moments, I reminded her that she has the chalice with her and further that *in a dream anything can happen.*

"I am very frightened even with the chalice but I am going down into the water. At first the water is light but as I get lower it becomes darker. There are all manner of fish swimming here. Now I see the grotto but cannot see the monster. Suddenly it appears from within the grotto. It looks like Godzilla. I quickly touch it with my chalice, taming it. This grotto has many other caves leading off it. All of them are quite empty but I am aware that there is light of some sort there. I reascend through the water and reach the ledge and remove the diving suit. The monster has followed me there so I touch it again with the chalice. It has begun to change in appearance ... Oh! It has turned into Mark". *(Mark is her boy friend).*

"... I have reascended the cliff and the mountain and begin climbing the stairway. The figure like grandfather is greeting me and congratulating me and handing me another scroll. The chalice is shining brightly. I descend the mountain and settle at the foot of it to rest awhile before undertaking my next mission".

Warren's Second Daydream (Case Ref. : S.164):

He selects the lighter diving gear, explaining that he always likes to travel light and not feel too encumbered.

Having spent most of his life in the Navy, Warren has no difficulties in descending into the deep water where he soon locates the grotto, which he describes in surprise as being quite dry and well-lit inside. The monster is aware of his presence and rears up on its hind legs just inside the entrance.

" The monster is grey-green in colour, big eyes, breathing fire, and has very sharp claws. The beast is standing on its hind legs and is more than three times my size. Its head is covered in bumps, horny. Its eyes are black. It has very wide teeth, vicious looking, squared at the top Its tongue is very red. It is a most unusual creature, like nothing I have seen before".

"I thrust at it with my sword not wishing to kill it but merely to subdue it. This seems to work because it is no longer breathing fire and has shrunk in size".

He swims back to the ledge but the monster has followed him so he taps it gently with the sword, whereupon it turns into ... Jessie *(his girl-friend).*

"Do you have any fear of her?"

"Yes, I am afraid that I shall not be able to *make it* with her".

"What do you mean?"

"She wants us to marry but I am frightened that I might be incapable of a happy union with her".

His subsequent ascent of the mountain is described as being "much easier".

Stuart's Second Daydream. (Case Ref.: T.68):

"I have descended into the water. The seabed is not as deep down as I had expected. I soon encounter the sea monster. It is like a large black snake. Using "excaliber" I subdue it easily. It had been coiled up on an old sea-chest, a chest that looks as if it might contain treasure. I want to take the chest with me but it is too heavy for me to manage on my own". I swim back to the rocky ledge and the serpent is following me so I touch it once again with excaliber ... Oh!"

"What has happened?"

"The serpent has changed into a girl!"

(Silence)

"Now what is happening?"

"I decided to go back for the treasure and have asked the girl to help me. She has agreed but even with the two of us it is really hard going."

He is obviously going through a struggle. Finally he breaks the silence:

"We have succeeded in getting the chest onto the ledge and together we are making the journey back up the mountain. The girl's hair is blowing in the wind as we ascend but I feel no wind at all upon my face or hair".

After ascending the stairway he is told by Jesus to open the chest and when he does so many birds fly out.

Again he finds it difficult to return to the *mundane level* below.

Beryl's Second Daydream (Case Ref. : W.154):-

She selected the lighter of the diving outfits so that she could travel more speedily. Descended with her eyes closed. (Symbolically: *was afraid of what she might discover*). There is a shutter across the entrance to the monster's grotto. (Again, symbolic *of hiding what might be beyond*) and the shutter is described as being "... solid, made of iron of great thickness ..."

(Silence)

"What is happening?"

"I don't want to go through this barrier".

"In a dream anything is possible ... "

(Silence)

"What is happening, are you through the barrier?"

"I can't get through the barrier".

"Why?"

"What is behind it is shutting me out".

(Silence)

"What is happening?"

"I feel out of breath. I must return to the surface".

"All right, return to the surface for a rest".

"Oh! I just had to come up for air".

"When you feel rested I want you to re-descend and have another attempt at going through that shutter. It is something you must do".

She descends again and encounters a very old man, dressed in black and carrying a stick and whose eyes are closed as if he is asleep. She asks him to open the shutter but he tells her that she is the only one who can open it. After a lapse of time she says that she has managed to force open the shutter but then tries to grasp hold of the shutter instead of entering the cave beyond.

"Let go! You have the Chalice to help you".

"I do not think that the chalice has the power in this situation. I believe that it is the old man who is the monster and he seems supernatural, not human, not of the world".

"Touch him with the chalice then and see what happens".

"I touch him with the chalice and now I suddenly realise that he is there to help me for it is *I* who is the monster!"

"Beyond the cave it is like my own house".

(Silence).

"Describe it!"

"It is like a black hole. There is no way out".

"In a dream anything is possible. Touch yourself with the chalice and see what happens".

"I have touched myself with the chalice and I have become two people, one is good and the other evil. I realise that I have to overcome the evil, which is very strong. I attempt to touch the evil me with the chalice but it is very strong and pushes me against the wall. At first I am powerless then I manage to press the chalice against the evil one and as I do so, it just melts away. Now all that remains is a black cloak and a stick".

She described her return to the mountain, her easy ascent of it and then the climb up the stairway beyond where she said that she was " ... met by a Higher Being, adorned in a pure white cloak and having a fire in front of him". She described how her chalice was transformed into a sword shaped like a cross. "... the blade is of finest silver and the hilt of purest gold and Jesus is upon the hilt thereof".

* * *

CHAPTER 7

"As we know, the parental image is constituted on the one hand by the personally acquired image of the personal parents, but on the other hand by the parent archetype which exists *a priori*, i.e. in the pre-conscious structure of the psyche." - Carl G. Jung, *Essays on Contemporary Events.*

In earlier Chapters we looked at the themes of the *First* and the *Second* Directed Daydreams. We discovered that in both instances a *basic law of the mind* is followed by Desoille in the use of his technique, that is, the client's movements are directed primarily in the vertical dimension, either as an *ascent* or as a *descent.* We also found that the *ascent,* although involving considerable effort at times by the client, usually evoked pleasant images, whereas a *descent* produced more sinister images. Although Jungian analysts will be familiar with these images, Desoille points out that this is only inasmuch "as they have arisen spontaneously from folklore traditions (and) they (the Jungian Analysts) have no methods for *intentionally* evoking them so that they can be studied *in vivo* and used therapeutically". In this context we examined the responses evoked by a dozen of my clients and we were able to see how each client had his or her unique method of overcoming the problems encountered. Sometimes the method was quite ingenious, quite imaginative.

We are now about to examine the themes of the Third and Fourth Daydreams. Once again, these daydreams involve a descent, in both instances *a descent into a cave*. However, there are differences in our approach to these two daydreams inasmuch as they have to be adapted according to the *sex* of the client. This adaptation is perhaps the first thing we notice about the *third* daydream: if the client is a man, then the daydream involves a descent into a cave to find a *witch* or *sorceress;* whereas if the client is a woman the descent into a cave is to find a *wizard* or *magician.* Later, when we take a look at the theme of Daydream 4, we discover that it has a very strong link with its preceding Daydream, and requires similar adaptation. In Daydream 4 it is the male client who has to descend into the cave of a wizard or a magician and the female client who has to descend into the cave of the witch or sorceress.

For purposes of illustration, the selected case histories are continued, although I have changed the order in which they appear. The female clients are shown first, following the same sequence as before; the male clients are also shown in sequence but grouped together and follow on after the females. From these illustrations it should be clear that the adaptations mentioned were given at the outset to each client. Although Directed Daydreams 3 and 4 are closely associated, limitation of space necessitates my giving each client's accounts of Daydream 3 and Daydream 4 quite separately, thus they are spread over this and the next Chapter. I would have preferred, in order to facilitate the reading of these illustrations, to have given each client's accounts of them as following one from the other although it is emphasised that the Daydreams are not condensed into one psychotherapy session and are spread over at least two sessions.

Anna's Third Daydream (Case Ref: G.118):

"The scroll tells me that my third assignment is to search for the cave of a wizard or sorcerer and go down into it and confront him.

"I descend the mountain without difficulty and make my way to the edge of the forest where I find a cottage. I knock upon the door of the cottage. The door is opened by an old man, who is tall and lean with white hair and white beard and white bushy eyebrows. However, his eyes look kindly at me. He takes me to some stables behind the cottage and invites me to select a horse for my journey. I select a deep chestnut. I journey through the forest and the pathway is very dark and narrow. The earth is very damp and I can hear water rushing nearby. I come to an oak tree at which point the path divides into two. Selecting the right hand path I proceed to where the wooded area becomes thinner and rocks abound. I find the cave tucked in the corner of some rocks, its floor slopes downwards and as it is too small to take the horse, I leave him outside and descend alone, fearfully. Suddenly I come across the Sorcerer who has a pointed head, pointed chin and is very small in height, about 3 ft. He has only one arm and although he has enormous feet, walks with a limp. He is wearing a black cloak. He has a yellow moustache. He is doing something with the fire ... he has seen me. I feel nervous for, although he turns his back to me, I feel that he is a threat. I am holding the chalice in front of me.

"I walk round him so that I can face him. He is looking into the fire. I feel powerless and rooted to the spot. I cannot move. It may be the Sorcerer's mind but I feel suffocated and the fire burns hotter and hotter. so that I can hardly breathe. My chest feels tight, like a vice. I cannot move my head or my body and I feel as if my body is sinking quite rapidly into a tunnel. I seem to have come to a stop now although I have gone a long way down. it is so dark, black, no light anywhere. Although I can feel the chalice I cannot see it. Now I can see a faint glow of light and I walk towards it— the light is from a light bulb in another tunnel. I pass this and go round a bend and all is darkness again. Where it is so dark and so uneven under foot, I stumble. It is a narrow tunnel and I am encountering numerous bends; there is no light anywhere. I transfer the chalice to my left hand. I can hear nothing, smell nothing, see nothing. I feel so isolated. Apart from the chalice I can't feel anything either. Ah! Now I can hear water nearby. The chalice is beginning to glow and to give light. I see a long tunnel shooting-off from the one I am in. I am going to take that route even though it is low and narrow. Oh! I am stuck. I can't move either way. The walls feel like rock but I am using the chalice to sort of burn or enlarge the area where I am standing. Now I am through the rock but into yet another tunnel. Water is coming into this one from the right. I am feeling so exhausted as it feels so tight. It is hard going. Now I have reached another tunnel where the water is. It is no larger but I stay with it for there is a light up ahead at a bend and I can hear birds. Now I have emerged into ... sunshine. I am in a ravine and I call to the horse. It responds to my call and is coming towards me over some very steep rocks. He makes it to my side and gratefully I am mounting him. He takes me back through the forest, back to the cottage and here I thank him and stable him. I reascend the mountain and soon reach its peak. The shaft of golden light is there and I ascend it until I meet a very elderly man with white hair, white beard, chubby cheeks, with a nice smile and such kindly, warm, loving eyes. I hand him the third scroll and accept from him the fourth. My chalice is bright yellow, lighter, inside it is silver."

Barbara's Third Daydream (Case Ref: C.133):

"The horse which I select to travel to the cave of the wizard is dapple-grey. As I ride through the woods the sun is glistening through the trees and all around is a pleasant, earthy, leaf-mould smell. I enter a cave in a clearing to the right of the woods. The Wizard or magician is inside but he is a pleasant-faced man, not unlike Merlin in appearance with snowy white hair and beard. He is wearing a cone-shaped hat with the shapes of the sun and moon embossed upon it. His whole appearance is glistening and he is kindly and welcoming. His eyes are blue, his skin pale. He greets me and takes my hand: I am aware that his hands are gentle and in no way do I feel threatened by him. I therefore talk to him as I believe that he can be reasoned with. In fact, the Magician tells me that he would like to go back with me and climb the mountain to the stairway in the sky. He "floats" up the mountain and the stairway and we meet the faceless one whom the Magician calls "the mighty one". Time is spent discussing my problems, with the Wizard taking on the role of "mediator". I am aware that my cup is now shining brightly and I am feeling very pleased with myself."

Eleanor's Third Daydream (Case Ref: F.19):

"It is now wintry at the top of the mountain but quite sunny at the tree line. I am having no difficulty in descending. At the foot of the mountain I discover a gingerbread cottage. I see a little old man, gnome-like, rosy-faced, bald-headed. He has four horses and they all look powerful and sleek. They are all reddish-black in colour and look almost mythological. I select one and as I mount it I am feeling somehow that I am confronting *myself!* There is a turbulent feeling, strong resistance but now I am astride him I am sensing the thrill of power. I feel that against this the Sorcerer's power will be ineffectual. It is night and I am bombarded by symbols: moons, stars, pentacles and other geometrical signs. There is an aura around my horse that has a silver bridle. All seems as if I have invested myself in magic. The branches of the trees are becoming thicker and meeting overhead making progress difficult. A mountain appears ahead of me and there is a storm playing around its peak. I gallop round to the other side of the mountain; it is like a moonscape, grey and barren; seemingly there is no life there, just inert and hostile and without water. Suddenly *steam,* no smoke, rises up from between the rocks. The horse's eyes are gleaming; he is strong; he is intrepid, calm and peaceful. I am finding it difficult to locate the sorcerer's cave ... ah! there it is. It is a small access and I shall have to bend down to enter it. The height does not permit the horse entering it so I have to go in alone. The chalice is in front of me, unsupported in mid-air and lights the path. Down and down, damp, wet, mossy and sulphurous and hot. it is getting hotter and hotter; he must be more of a devil than a sorcerer. Now there are flames at the bottom. I feel that there is something I have to do and I am reminded of the protection I have been given of the chalice and the horse. The horse guards the exit; the chalice is inviolate; nothing can overcome it. I see the Sorcerer ... he is busy making some evil mixture over a table, from the directions in an old book. He is perusing the book while holding it in one hand the fingers of which are gnarled and have very long nails; whilst stirring the contents of a pot with something clasped in his other hand. Scattered around are bones and mummified things. How dirty his hands are. He is wearing a hat and a cloak. He has a big nose. He is ancient, wrinkled and smelly ... he smells rotten, bad. He is bent with age. He is of medium build. He is wearing boots under his cloak and a sort of black jerkin, full of holes. His hair is long and tangled and matted and dirty. His eyes are like Marty Feldman's! He is aware of my presence. Bats are flying around but they do not worry me as I like bats. He is muttering in an aggressive and irritated tone ... a monologue. Although nasty, he is pathetic. He is annoyed that the storm, which he threw up, did not touch me. He looks over his left shoulder and his face looks more frightening. I sense that when he is looking in this way it gives him more power, focuses his being. His face is greyish-white and very evil. He is making the potion more noxious. He is trying to attack me but is powerless against the Chalice. There is a stalemate and then the horse appears, dashes forward and holds the sorcerer. I am now moving to his right with the Chalice which illuminates a lot of people who are petrified and in their stone appear like Greek classical statues - men, women and children - there are dozens of them, two deep in the corridor. What is needed to release these figures? *A TRANSFORMATION OF THE WIZARD.* The horse is trying to tell me something. it has a power, which is manifested in a gold star in orb in its mane. I retrieve it and it now appears on top of the horse's head. I pick up the star and advance on the sorcerer who is now cowering down - now he is on his knees and he seems to be getting smaller and smaller and disappears in a puff of smoke. In his place is a young man in princely clothes. To me he represents a primary masculine figure, very handsome though. The stone falls off the captives and they are released. They seem to be members of the Prince's Kingdom. Why had the Prince become the Sorcerer? It was *EVIL* within themselves which changed them all and which needed a *GOOD* force to release them. With the transition, the whole area has changed to a field, rustic scenery, warmth. It is May-time, a village, all transformed. Reopened to the *LIFE.*

"I journey back to the cottage at the foot of *the* mountain where I return the horse to the gnome. I reascend the mountain, gaining the top easily. As I begin to ascend the stairway I meet a figure descending - tall, well-built, curly brown hair close to his head, high forehead, very benign. I report what has happened. My chalice is still effervescent but has jewels in its shining silver stem and base, which is square. He hands me the scroll for my next assignment but once again I am permitted rest in the cave with the Owgle; this place has become a solid representation of home".

This session brought her several cognitions about the ANIMA and the ANIMUS and the female child within her. She said that she had experienced an inner awakening and her original problems no longer seemed to have importance because they are of the OUTER only. She said that after writing up the Daydream she realised this and felt that it is the INNER marriage and ultimate spiritual orgasm that really counts.

Anita's Third Daydream (Case Ref: G.93):

"From my resting place at the foot of the mountain, I went to a small thatched cottage on the edge of the distant wood. The door was opened by a man resembling *my father*, even to the shirt and trousers he was wearing. I was taken to a stable where I chose a chestnut horse, rejecting the black and grey and white ones. I rode to a distant cave. Following a red glow, I walked down into the cave. A sorcerer wearing a blue and black outfit was dancing in one place. My assignment was to confront and calm this person. I held up my vessel; he was surprised. I changed his book of spells into a Bible. I collected a pair of sunglasses for him and wearing these he was able to come out into the sunlight with me. I returned the horse and the man resembling my father was pleased to see me back. On reascending the mountain and the stairway beyond my vessel was very light green but went white in sunlight. The Angel Being seemed quite satisfied."

Rita's Third Daydream (Case Ref: M.37):

"I descend the mountain with no problems - flying from rock to rock. I make my way to a cottage at the edge of the forest. There is a man dressed all in brown. He is not big but wiry and strong. He reminds me of an acorn with the potential power of the mighty oak. His eyes are hazel-grey, deep-set in a wrinkled face that has bushy eyebrows; his hair and his beard are mousy-grey in colour. In the stable adjoining the cottage are three horses : a black, a heavy dapple-grey and a white with plumes. I have selected the dapple-grey and set off on my journey through the forest. The sun is shining and everywhere looks very pretty. After a while I come to a large oak tree and sense that I have accomplished about half my journey. The forest on the other side of the oak seems darker. I press on and as I approach the far edge of the forest I notice that it becomes lighter. Now I have emerged from the trees and ahead of me is a cave with a very wide entrance although a large rock obscures the cave's natural opening to the left. There is a blue-purple glow in the darkness beyond. The ground is very uneven. Inside the cave there are bats flying about; they are singing. The cave narrows and yet is illuminated by light from above - a window cut into the hillside. The passage I am following curves round and now there are some steps going down. I can smell a fire - an acrid, yet somehow pleasant smell. The floor at the bottom of the passage is made of brick. A man is sitting on a three-legged stool beside a cauldron to the right side of the room. He looks dark. There are homemade cupboards around the room with windows to the left. The man is unaware of my presence. On one windowsill is a reptile, a green lizard with a very red inside to its mouth. The man is dressed in a dark cloak, tied around the middle and the cloak has a hood or a cowl like that of a monk. ... He has seen me now as he has stood up and turned to face me. He now looks quite tall and is younger than I originally thought. He has a strong but kindly face. Somehow I do not feel threatened by him; he is more like a friend, a teacher. He has a big face and head, brown eyes, brown wavy hair, big nose and laughter on his lips. He has invited me to lunch and I have decided to stay. He seems surprised that someone has come down to see him. Now something is happening outside; a storm with blue light is coming through the window — almost like a beam of blue light. Now it withdraws. Suddenly I feel that I want to jump into this light and he wants to join me and go out through the window with me but as I jump into the blue light it pulls me out alone. I am now standing on the hillside. I whistle for my horse, mount him and make my way back to the cottage, feeling exhilarated. I return the horse to the old man who is waiting at the gate and gives the horse an apple. I ascend the mountain and make the peak easily as I feel so full of energy. I ascend the stairway shaft. The figure I meet descending it is oriental with a pigtail and red robes, a bit faded but still splendid with a gold waist-girdle around. He is also wearing gold sandals. He is quite plump but very, very kind. I return the Third Scroll to him and take the Fourth from him. My Chalice is giving out a green light right from its centre; the outer is unchanged in shape but there is ... like a bird behind it with wings outstretched - sort of dark purple. The bird belongs to the man and it is now sitting on his left shoulder and is white. The Chalice now has an emerald in its cup, bigger than the sapphire. I decide once again to remain on the mountain top before embarking on the Fourth mission".

The interpretation of this daydream will be looked at in a later chapter but at this point of her treatment she remarked that the shaking, from which she had formerly suffered, had shown much improvement and that she was feeling much better generally including a considerable improvement in her sense of balance.

Sylvia's Third Daydream (Case Ref: M.164):

"I am given the scroll by the man on the mountain and proceed on my journey. My mission is to overcome the Sorcerer in his cave. I call at a cottage and adjacent to it is a stable containing several horses of varying colours. I select a brown horse that I mount and at a trot we make our way through the forest. Nothing eventful takes place during the journey although from the appearance of the trees I imagine that it is Autumn time. I soon spy the Sorcerer's cave, dismount and enter it on foot. As soon as I see the Sorcerer I am aware of his extreme power even though he is not threatening me in any way. He looks, at first, a little like the Sorcerer in *"The Sorcerer's Apprentice"*. however, this picture soon fades as his presence becomes more threatening. He is wearing a hat and cloak of dark, blue-black colour. His long hat has the pointed top squashed down a little. He is bearded but at one point he becomes featureless and then becomes many faces, changing constantly to Edward, my brother Edward, my brother-in-law, James. All these faces are appearing and disappearing. His hands are incidental to the whole situation and I am finding it difficult describing them at all. At one time his fists are clenched and it is difficult to see whether he is holding something in his hand. After a time I make out what he is holding - it is a knife. As I look closely, I see that he is grinning; he does not seem at all worried by the Chalice. I am supposed to confront him and presumably overcome him but to me this is an impossibility as I feel that he is very aware of why I am here and that I am not capable because he is all-powerful. He is almost daring me to challenge him, knowing that I will fail. It is as if he doesn't find it necessary to threaten me in any way because it makes no difference, he will overcome me anyway.

"I feel powerless and weak, tired of the thought of trying. At this point I am facing him and feel completely on my own, alone without any defence. I sit down as I am so weak and cannot do anything. This may not be wise but it doesn't seem to matter to me because I have no energy to do anything. He is looking at me and then *consumes me.* I don't know how or what happens. I cannot see him or feel him. Apart from my overwhelming despair I don't feel anything. The rest is a blur until I look for the Chalice, which is gone. I don't care where it is, it doesn't matter. I feel I just want to go to sleep".

I prompt her to look for the Chalice.

"Now I see it in his hand!"

I prompt her to get it back, reminding her that anything is possible in a dream.

"How I get it back I don't remember or how I get out of the cave but when I do he is with me at my back on the horse. I make my way back to the mountain with him on my back and struggle up the mountain with him still on my back. The monk takes the Sorcerer off my back and I show him the Chalice, which looks grubby, rusty sort of green until the sun shines on it. Even then it isn't the same but I cannot be bothered to care how it looks. Even when the Sorcerer is taken off my back I don't even feel relief. How could the monk have allowed it to happen?

"I accept the new scroll for my next mission and return to the top of the mountain".

Following this daydream, she had a massive emotional release whilst at the cinema with her boy friend, Jamie. Afterwards she felt exhausted, slept and felt fine when she awoke. Throughout the week she was less work-conscious, treating things more lightly and chatting with the girls she normally supervised.

Michaela's Third Daydream (Case Ref: O.45):

"I set off for a cottage on the edge of the forest. It is a little white cottage with black windows; there are little love-hearts cut into it! The garden is full of red and white roses. I knock at the cottage door and a man answers the door. He seems like my father but doesn't resemble him in appearance at all. He leads me to a stable where there are three horses—a black one, a grey-white one and a golden-brown one. I take the black one. I mount up and make my way through the forest and arrive at a large oak tree. The path goes either side of the oak so I decide to take the right hand path. There are two people walking in the forest. They are complete strangers, a male and a female, both in their twenties I should think. They just look at me as I ride past them. I journey on until I see a cave from which there is a red glow. The forest is dark here and there are no sounds of birds; it is evening time. I feel scared. As I reach the cave I see that a glow is coming from way back inside. I leave the horse and go ahead on foot. A wizard stands there throwing things into a cauldron and talking in a foreign language. He is old, thin, tall. He has a white beard but he is very gaunt and his face is drawn in; his eyes are an odd bluish-brown. He has seen me but chooses to ignore me. I have the chalice but approach him very cautiously. His hand is long with long fingers and nails and it reaches out towards me. I put the chalice between us. Now *he is backing away* ... he is frightened! I touch him with the chalice, he vanishes.

"This cave is really quite interesting; there is weird writing on the walls and there are cobwebs all around. There is an open book, covered with dust; the book is written in a foreign language and full of symbols. There are many pots around too but nothing here I want. I decide to leave and find my horse, which I mount and start back through the night forest. An owl is hooting. I feel very confident somehow although the night is dark and the forest creepy. How different things are in the dark but my horse is so sure-footed! There, now, is the cottage. I knock on the door and tell the man that I am returning the horse. I explain the outcome of my mission and then climb the mountain on foot. I feel very lonely and I cannot see properly and have to *feel* my way up. I feel tired and would like to rest but I keep climbing. Ow! I have scratched my leg, my left leg. What a nasty graze but I must keep on up. Now, at last I have reached the top. I can just make out the outline of the stairs and slowly and carefully climb them. The man who looks like my grandfather greets me. He is extremely pleased with me and congratulates me. I take the 4th scroll from him and hold up the chalice, which is shining brightly. Now, as I descend, the stairway is half-lighted. It is dark as I go down the mountain but as I get to the foot it is slowly getting lighter as I see the sun rising over the opposite side of the mountain. I can see the rocks clearly now and I have reached the base where there is a shack with some bedding and food where I can rest awhile".

Beryl's Third Daydream (Case Ref: W.154):

There was a lapse of five or six weeks between the second and third daydreams because of the Christmas holiday and subsequent bad weather during January which made it impossible for Beryl to motor in to see me. On beginning the third daydream she insisted on going back up the stairway to meet the Higher Being.

"The Higher Being is now adorned in a pure white cloak and has a fire in front of him. As I raise my chalice towards him it becomes transformed into a sword, shaped like a cross with a large hilt on which Jesus appears. The handle of the sword is of pure gold; its blade, pure silver".

She sets off on the next assignment and goes down the mountain in an escalator! After this she walks to the edge of the wood (forest) and finds the cottage where she is greeted by a man dressed in a monk's grey habit. She selects a black horse and travels to the cave of the Sorcerer. Dismounting, she enters the cave and describes it thus:

"There are false gods painted on the walls of the cave with Arab or Egyptian symbols but these do not disturb me in any way. A green pool of water casts a green glow like a light and I feel good about this. It seems to be a controlling factor for any evil here. In fact, I feel there is no point in actually confronting the Sorcerer since he is *already controlled"*

This is particularly interesting since in her second daydream she had already overcome the Archetypal Father, ahead of schedule!

"I return to the cottage and leave the horse there. The monk follows me and ascends the mountain with me. When we reach the summit, I am unable to ascend the stairway because there is an evil smoke on the stairway, ugly and waiting to destroy".

Asked to describe it, she replied:

"It is big, green, evil and oriental".

She describes how she attempts to use the sword against it but finds that the sword is too heavy for her to lift with her right hand.

I tell her to use ***both*** *hands.*

"Now the sword has broken in two!"

I tell her to use the broken sword.

"Yes, I am doing that. The evil is actually a serpent that has now become surrounded in a bright light and I am able to step over it. I make my way to a beautiful golden temple where I am permitted to rest".

Her own interpretation of this was that the serpent represented her own evil side. She then went on to talk about her late father, an alcoholic, whom she had begun to accept and love, when he was knocked down by a drunken motorcycle gang on a pedestrian crossing. She said that her father had been put on a life-support machine but was "like a cabbage" and she had to convey the decision to discontinue the life-support as there was no real chance of his recovery. There was a tremendous release of emotion (abreaction).

Colin's Third Daydream (Case Ref: L.70):

"After selecting a grey horse and journeying to the cave, I find the Sorceress standing in front of a large cage in which there are some twenty or so captives, all chained. She warns me to keep away but makes no attempt to harm me. However, when I ignore her warning and move in closer she jumps up and down in rage and shouts at me. I draw closer to her and again she threatens me but does nothing. When I touch her, she calms down and even allows me to take the keys from her and unlock the cage and release all the captives from their chains. All the former captives are turning around and going out of the cave. At this point, she uses her powers, which are like a magnet, and takes my sword away from me. She then proceeds to lock all the captives in again and laughs as she walks to another part of the cave where she puts my sword away. The grey horse is outside so I whistle to it but the sorceress is using a magic force like an electric field and the horse runs away. I have decided to enlist the help of the prisoners and we are all sitting down together to formulate a plan. Although the cage is quite strong, a concerted effort by all could force it open. It works! A gap is made large enough for them all to slip through one at a time. The prisoners in this way all make good their escape while the grey horse comes back to keep the sorceress occupied. I am able to creep into the other part of the cave and retrieve my sword. I then climb onto the grey horse and we make good our escape. The Sorceress tries to follow us at first but then gives up the chase.

I gallop back through the forest and after returning the grey horse to the stables, re-ascend the mountain and the stairway beyond where I meet the Pure Light. I raise my sword in salute whereupon it shines brightly as before".

Carl's Third Daydream (Case Ref: M.130):

On his descent of the mountain he encounters brambles that do not seriously impede his progress but are nevertheless irritating. He is then attacked by a black dog, which grips his left arm. Finally manages to free himself from the dog but later encounters a bear, which has to be fought off with the *curved sword.* He describes how he eventually finds the cave of the witch but is warned by a male knight on a white horse not to enter it. He disregards this warning and enters the cave. The place is full of bats and the floor of the cave besides going downwards also winds round and round. The witch is beside her cauldron and is described as being " ...an old hag, grotesque features and dressed entirely in black".

She asks him if he wants anything from her cauldron to which he replies with an emphatic "No!" He feels that she is "a threat, a very evil one" and he decides that he must rid himself of her, kill her. However, he feels that she is aware of his intentions and is continuing to keep a very wary eye on him.

He describes how, suddenly, holes appear in the side of the cave and some seven or eight little devils appear with pitchforks. To this new threat he faces up squarely and uses the straight sword, killing most of them. He says that the witch summoned these up to her aid but realises that such attempts are futile. She is angry and waves her arms about sending all manner of manifestations at him but he is able to stand up to all of these. Finally, the witch "crumples up and I am able to detach myself from her influence".

On his return to the mountain through the forest he is again attacked by bats that he has to beat off. He reaches the base of the mountain feeling very tired and its ascent proves difficult as the climb itself is a struggle in his exhausted state. Finally he makes the summit and when he meets the old man in the white robes on the stairway he discovers that the straight sword is glowing brightly.

Warren's Third Daydream (Case Ref: S.164):

"I descend the mountain rapidly, encountering no difficulties. I make my way to a stable beside a cottage and select from among the horses a brown one with a white nose. My journey to the cave of the witch is on the edge of the forest and the path is very hilly. I see the entrance to the witch's cave and enter it still on my horse. The cave is wide and the slope downwards ends in a very bright area at the bottom. The witch is just standing there; very bent and very old and I do not see her as representing any threat to me at all. She has some gnomes there with her that she has held in a cage as prisoners but although I set them all free and tell them to go, I feel that they should have freed themselves. As I leave the cave I notice that the old witch is staring at the empty cage. Although she poses no real threat to me somehow I feel that she is upset by my leaving her.

"I return to the cottage and an old lady there tells me to put the horse with the white nose back into the stables and then to come into the cottage where she is cooking a meal for me".

"After resting a while, I re-ascend the mountain with no problem and ascend to the 4th stair. I notice that my sword is glowing around the edges ..."

Stuart's Third Daydream (Case Ref: T.68):

He sets off on the third mission on a white horse which he selects and begins the journey in search of the witch's cave. The journey is fraught with many obstacles, tree roots that nearly trip his horse, branches across his path, etc.,. At last he sees the cave, describing it as being "on a slope between two gently sloping hills". When he attempts to enter the cave, however, he meets up with an invisible barrier and cannot get through. After several attempts, he decides to try entering the cave *backwards* and in this way manages somehow to get through the barrier. The witch, a middle aged attractive woman, is just inside the cave. Stuart finds it necessary to hold onto the wall to stop her forcing him back and then realises that he cannot use his sword because his sword hand is encumbered! Behind the witch is a red glow and he feels that in some way his presence is helping to kindle the witch's fire. She takes hold of his sword and holds it in her hand. Stuart is surprised by the strength of her grip. However, he eventually manages to twist it free, cutting her hand in the process. She smiles at him, which makes him suspicious as he feels it is a trick. He tries to stamp out the fire and after much effort succeeds but it immediately rekindles. This happens again but eventually he pours water over it from a cauldron and then stands on the fire.

In the cave he sees some captives whom he releases but does not feel particularly happy about doing so. The witch is angry and seems to be ageing. Suddenly she goes for his throat and he begins to choke. He does not want her to hit her head and so holds her close to him instead so that she cannot choke him. Then the cave becomes bathed in daylight and the witch is burned up by this.

His mission accomplished, he begins the journey back but there are branches to contend with and obstacles on the path. Finally reaches the stable but the white horse is reluctant to go into the stable. He ascends the mountain and the stairway beyond, where the figure of Jesus, the Christ stands. However, Jesus is now more female in appearance. He reports what took place and is about to raise his sword in salutation when he notices that it is a bit rusty but he allows the sun to shine upon its blade and that cleans it. The sword hilt—the part of the sword that he holds— has not changed

He has to lean forward to get back down the stairway and notices that he is wearing new shoes ... no! Old shoes!

CHAPTER 8

I am part of all that I have met: yet all experience is an arch wherethro' gleams that untravll'd world. - **Tennyson**

We continue our examination of the twelve clients' accounts of *Daydream 4;* which it will be seen is similar to *Daydream 3* in that it is varied according to the sex of the client. Thus, with Daydream 4, for male clients it involves a descent into a cave to confront a *wizard* or *sorcerer* and with females, a descent into the cave of a *witch* or *sorceress.*

Anna's Fourth Daydream (Case Ref: G.118):

"The scroll tells me that my fourth assignment is to search for the cave of a witch or sorceress, descend into her cave and confront her.

"I set off from the cave in the mountain and reach a cottage on the edge of a forest. The cottage has a thatched roof but has very dirty walls and dirty windows. The door is brown. I knock on the door and after a short wait the door is opened by a woman who resembles my mother. She leads me to a stable behind the house where there are two horses. The first of these is big, brown with a white tail. The second is smaller and jet-black. I select the black one and ride him into the forest. The forest soon becomes dark and I feel frightened. Eventually I reach a large oak tree where the path I'm on divides into two, one path leading to the left of the oak and another to its right. I select the left path. I am surprised to find that my journey is quite hilly in places but the horse pulls well and eventually I reach the edge of the forest. The edge of the forest is rocky and the trees are sparse. I see several caves but the cave of the witch has a red glow coming from it. I dismount and leave my horse on the outside of the cave while I enter the cave. It is very cramped inside with many dark corners. I am making my way along a little passageway and at the far end of this is a room from where the red glow comes. The witch is standing there looking at me. Behind her, in the corner of the room, is the brilliant red light. The witch is an old woman, thin, very mean and hard looking. She has thin, scraggy hair, very unkempt. She is dressed in a long black skirt, red blouse, deep red cloak with a fur collar. She is trying to take me over with a sort of hypnotic stare, gradually drawing me closer and closer to her. Although I fear her I raise my chalice up and point it towards her. As soon as I do this the magnetic, drawing power, which she had, is lessening and I know that she is losing her power. Now she has sat down. She is no longer a problem to me and I have no wish to kill her. A yellow light seems to be coming from one side of the room so I walk towards it to examine it closer. The light is actually coming from a mesh window. In the small room beyond is a little girl about 3 years old and very pretty. She looks very frightened. I now see another window, similar to the first, and in the room beyond this is an old man fast asleep. He looks very bent and I judge him to be about 90. I now see a corridor with yet another window although this one is not so light I can make out two fair-haired little boys in the room beyond, ages about 5 and 7. They are obviously very frightened because they are consoling one another. The younger of the two is crying for his mother. I am conscious that it is very dark here and there is mud underfoot. In places the water is quite deep and I am aware that the water is trickling down the walls to form a sort of pond in the middle of the room. It feels very cold. I go round the pond and suddenly find a woman of about 25 - 30 is there. She could be the mother of the children as she too is fair, light skinned. Actually her skin has an unhealthy pallor as if she hasn't seen the sun for a very long time. She is tied to a stake but I set her free and she tells me that the two little boys are her children and that the old man is her grandfather and he has been a prisoner there a long, long time. I lead them all out of the cave and notice as I do so that the red glow in the witch's cave is caused by a fairy light that I extinguish with the use of the vessel or chalice. This has the effect of transferring light to the chalice and I am able to light the way out of the cave like this. Once outside, I help the old man onto the black horse's back and then all of us make our way to the village where the old man, the woman and the two children live. I bid them all farewell and then mount the horse myself and journey back to the cottage on the edge of the forest where I return the black horse to its stable and make my way on foot to the mountain. I reascend it and find it easier to climb than before, even to the very peak. I climb the golden stairway and on the 12th stair meet God. He accepts the third scroll from me and hands me the fourth one. I raise the vessel in salutation. It is now silver, very, very shiny as if the sun shines on it. It is so shiny that is resembles polished chrome. I descend to the top of the mountain where I decide to rest for shelter; food, drink, blankets and a fire have been provided for my comfort".

Barbara's Fourth Daydream (Case Ref: C.133):

"Again I select the dapple-grey horse on which to travel to the cave of the witch. The route is more like that of a country park than of a dense forest. I discover a single cave, the inside of which is very dark, illuminated by a single red lantern. I enter the cave and descend into its depths. The witch is like Medusa with 20 or more snakes, her appearance is distorted and ugly and she is crawling along towards me. I quickly move round her, averting my eyes but I manage to touch her with the cup on the back of her head whereupon she disintegrates. This part of the cave is cone-shaped and smelly and I want to get back outside as quickly as possible, I return to the mountain, ascend it with no difficulty. The faceless man is now dressed in a bib and tucker. My vessel is quite bright."

Eleanor's Fourth Daydream (Case Ref: F.19):

"On leaving the mountain, I make my way to a thatched cottage by a stream. The cottage has a little front door. There is an old woman there. She looks like a witch. Ah! She looks like an old lady I once saw on a journey I made with Carol (my daughter) - gnarled hands, very old. This woman is in charge of the horses of which there are many but they are all different in appearance - but ordinary. There are greys, chestnuts, bays, dark ... I select a chestnut, mount it and ride off. The forest is green but dense, forming a high canopy. This is a very old wild wood. I reach the edge of it where I see some rocks. there is a hole in the ground with a red glow coming from it. I dismount, placing my feet in the big silver stirrups. The mouth of this cave is perpendicular and it is very hot. The way in, the entrance, is a barrier. I look around for help. In the distance I see Merlin. He is now handing me a rope ladder, which is not affected by the heat. I hold up the Chalice, which acts as a cloak all around me. I am descending the ladder; down, down and down. At the bottom is a pit of leaping flames. There is a platform around the edge of the pit. "one foot at a time, friend" echoes in my ears. I edge carefully round it in this way and then it broadens out. As I look around, I am aware that it is incredibly hot and very bright, a flickering brightness. Now I can see an image of the old witch and she looks like the Queen in *Snow-white*—beautiful, haughty, demanding. It is like a hologram of her. There is a lot of black magic and power, which has a fatal attraction. *She* is more powerful than the Sorcerer; she uses illusory magic. The image is to deflect me from meeting her. Her substance is anything she wants it to be. She has many personas or images and can change to animal, human or the elements but in a negative sense. Her power attracts me and I am beginning to comprehend the enormity of her magic. She has no form, only a malevolent force. She is everywhere and nowhere simultaneously.

"The Chalice is giving out a strong blue light. She is subscribing a circle around me — the power is small but impregnable. she is wind, bats, malevolence, a witch. There is real anger. She is trying to destroy — howling, screaming, which is rising to a crescendo.

"Suddenly it is all silent; all the force is gone and there is stillness. Then a voice asks: "What are you here for?" It is haughty but imperious as if we have reached a stalemate. However, I feel apprehensive but I do not know what to do. Suddenly the ground shifts beneath me and I am falling down, down into icy cold water. Horrible laughter follows me down. The water is green and there is a strong current pulling me along faster and faster - rapids! waterfalls! The breath is knocked out of me. now the water levels out to a still lake and I move to a rocky slope that I clamber up. It is good to rest.

"Then I am aware that this is still the witch's territory. I sense that the witch is inquisitive because I have survived. There is a sort of silent questioning — as if the inquisitiveness has overcome the malevolence causing a slight softening of attitude. Ahead of me are steps cut into the rock and I begin climbing up and up. I feel exhausted. One side is open to a precipice; thinking about the Owlet helps me to ascend. At the top is a small aperture leading into a golden cave. The witch is sitting on a golden throne and is herself gold - a mass of gold. Very modern-looking, magical looking. She is on a dais with steps leading up; it is her inner sanctum. She is demanding to know why I am here. She wants to know, to understand, what my power is for, who I am. There is a feeling of fear, affinity, respect ... mutual respect. Her power is equal to the Chalice but not of the same order. The Chalice is pouring out gold and inside it there is a mixture of gold and silver. I feel that this potion is very strong and more than equalling the witch's golden radiance. There is now a great radiance from the Chalice and it floods over the Queen who diminishes in size. She is no longer awe-inspiring, rather she seems more human. I see a curtained-off area to my right and I go through it, then up a narrow passage whose slope is gentle. The only light is from the Chalice. Now I am outside again where the horse is already waiting. I mount up and we trot back to the cottage where I return the horse and then reascend the mountain to its peak and then climb the golden stairs. The angel is here and the Chalice has even a greater light. I am instructed to descend to the mountain again and rest at its base ready for my next assignment".

This Daydream gave her insight into the ARCHETYPAL MOTHER and her relationship with her own mother symbolised by the confrontations in the Directed Daydream.

Anita's Fourth Daydream (Case Ref: G.93):

From my resting-place I went forth this time to a "square" cottage on the far side of the wood. The lady answering the door wore a light blue blouse and dark fawn skirt. Once again I chose a chestnut horse, leaving the grey and the white and rode to three distant caves. In the right hand cave was a sorceress, bent over a cauldron ... it was my mother! She was using spiders, bats and snakes. She threw a snake at my feet but it shrivelled when I threw a stone from my vessel onto it. I calmed her by throwing a stone into her cauldron. I did not want to strip her of her power. She came outside with me. She cried when I was about to leave so I took her back to the cottage. Inside the cottage, she sat quietly and let me make tea. Although I invited her to do so, she would not come to the mountain with me. I felt that there was a barrier between us that we had both made but I also felt that the woman no longer held any power over me. So I went back to the mountain alone. I ascended the mountain and climbed the stairway into the clouds to meet the Angel. My vessel was green again but once again in the sunlight became white with a thin gold rim."

Her real-life relationship with her mother was discussed at some length following which Anita seemed to be much more together as a person, having come to terms with her relationship with her mother.

Rita's Fourth Daydream (Case Ref: M.37):

"Again, my descent of the mountain is easy. I travel to the cottage and knock on the door. This time the door is opened by an old woman ... she seems very old yet somehow sort of ageless. She is wearing glasses. At times she looks quite young; at others very old indeed. She is wearing an apron. When she changes into a younger person she becomes tall, blond and nice looking; she has green eyes. I select a strong looking bay horse for my journey this time and mounting it, begin my journey. When I reach the oak tree where the forest path divides, I take the left-hand fork this time. The sky is overcast but the birds are singing. It is a summer's day but not hot. At the oak, however, it becomes sunnier and the sunlight is making the ground bright and I see many little animals. Eventually I come to the edge of the forest and immediately see the cave. I dismount, tie my horse to a bush outside the entrance to the cave and notice that the horse is very restless, nervous. There is a red glow from the cave and at first I experience a reluctance to proceed any further but manage to overcome my fear and I enter the cave. The red glow has changed to a pinkish hue on the left hand side of the cave but remains a smoky-red on the right. The earth is black and there are red flowers with no leaves, just stems. The cave is now becoming very narrow, merely a passage; it is now so narrow that I have to squeeze my way along it sideways. At the end of the passage is daylight coming through windows. I see an old woman in long clothes, a scrubbed table, a black kitchen range on the right with brass candlesticks on a mantelpiece immediately above the range. The old woman is bending over a candle. A solid wooden 16th century rocking-chair is her seat. The woman is old before her time but her features are gentle. Her head is swathed in shawls and things that cover also her shoulders and the upper part of her body although she is wearing a blue undergarment and a white apron. The shawls appear to be beige in colour. The woman has picked up a baby and gives it to me. The baby is quite tiny with brown hair. It is very placid and of sweet countenance. The woman has crossed to the window; she is holding a wooden staff in her hand and making some sort of salutation to the sun and the stars. There is something nasty under the table ... a revolting old crone who is crawling out to get the baby. The woman at the window addresses me and says "Give her the baby!" I obey. The old crone takes the baby gently from me, this is part of the other woman; the old crone is changing and the woman at the window is fading ... like energy going from one to the other. What was the crone is now a youngish, strong, black-haired woman. This is the Sorceress. She replaces the baby in its cradle. The walls appear to be of yellow sandstone and a dog is tied up by one wall. I release him and he jumps up happily; it is a round-faced shaggy sheepdog. The woman angrily tells me to take the dog away. I leave and take the dog with me but as I enter the narrow passageway I feel a sense of panic. I am afraid of getting stuck and I am also afraid of the Sorceress. However, I finally get through and reaching the mouth of the cave, *un-tether* my horse, which I proceed to mount, and at a gallop retrace my way back through the forest with the dog running swiftly beside me. When we get back to the cottage, the woman there takes the horse from me. The dog walks away into the forest alone. I make my way back to the mountain which is now clad in a carpet of heather. The ascent of the mountain is all right except that the peak is difficult as there is an overhang to negotiate. However, surprisingly, this presents no real problem ... it is almost as if someone unseen is helping me. Yes! There is, a strong but shadowy male figure like an Ancient god. I ascend the golden shaft stairway and meet a small, agitated man with white hair and moustache, like Sir George Trevelyan. He seems to think that I am late. He is dressed in dark blue robes. He says: "My dear, I thought you were never coming". He wants me to attend a feast. Before my eyes there appears a lot of complicated oriental Persian patterns in blue and turquoise and in the midst of them a golden table with people sitting around it. The person at the head of the table who looks a little like Henry VIII, says: "You have brought her too soon. Take her away!" A woman dressed in white is seated a little further down - an embodiment of gentleness though very poor. The impression which forms in my mind is that the *man* seems to be out of place - he is really a priest but is over-masculine - yet, a fine figure will emerge from Henry VIII's outer appearance to reveal a Priest in white with a shaven head. I hand the 4th scroll to the woman who, in turn, hands me the 5th. The Chalice is shedding purple light and the woman is looking delighted for the Chalice is of gleaming gold. I decide to remain at the peak of the mountain for awhile where all is bathed in purple light."

Sylvia's Fourth Daydream (Case Ref: M.164):

"As I am told to in the scroll, I make my way to a cottage which has a log grey wooden door. I batter this door as I seem to have difficulty in making anyone hear. A woman eventually opens it. She looks just like my mother! She allows me to select a horse, a palomino from the three that are there, the others being a salt-peppered colour, and a chestnut brown. I mount up and journey through the countryside. I am riding towards a sort of semi-circle of rocks and there are three caves. The middle one has a red glow coming from it. I dismount and enter the cave, which has a sloping floor. In spite of the glow it seems very dark in here. I am aware that the witch is watching me but not saying anything. Now I see her! She is old and is wearing a long dress of dark green. She has something wrapped round her hand. Her eyes are horrible — ugly, powerful, penetrating and wicked eyes. She is now changing her face to my mother's, then changes back. She turns away from me and goes round a corner. It is so very dark. I can't see but the witch can".

I suggest that the Chalice might help.

"Yes, oh yes, the Chalice is giving out light. Now the witch is cowering, trying to avoid me. She is in a recess and is keeping her distance. I *could* throw the Chalice at her. I am keeping my eyes on the witch. The witch is warning me through telepathy — a challenge. Although I am apprehensive, I am not going to turn back. *Ugh!* Rats have appeared and are scrambling round my feet. I bend down and scoop them up in my Chalice. The witch has her back to me for a moment. She is close enough for me to throw my arms round her but instead I am putting the chalice on the witch's head. Her whole head is under it. I am now taking her outside to the horse and I tie her to it. I am now leading the horse back through the forest to the cottage. I would like to tie the witch up for I know the woman couldn't control her. I would like to pull the chalice right over her but I cannot get it past her shoulders. If I push too much she will fight me. She is immobilised but I can't get the Chalice over her. She knows that I can't leave her. I decide to leave her tied to the horse and proceed to the mountain. The woman in the cottage is watching me all the time and somehow this is making me slow down; making me feel guilty. "I can't go" the Sorceress is moaning in a nagging voice. I am just standing here not knowing what to do".

"Anything is possible ... do something!"

"I go back to say goodbye to the woman. Now she wants me to stay! I feel trapped by this woman (*her mother).* I stay that night but leave in the morning and climb the mountain with the Sorceress while the woman watches me. At last I have reached the top. The monk is there, Now the witch is *absorbed into him.* I feel a desire to drink from the Chalice and do so. It contains red wine. The Chalice is unaltered in appearance. I accept the scroll for my next assignment and slowly descend the mountain".

This was a very difficult session for Sylvia. She had obviously been very much under her mother's influence. She described an incident where she was playing with some girls and they were dressing up in some old clothes; she was directing the game (she was 7 at the time). One point in the game involved tying up one of the girls. Her mother hid the old clothes up afterwards and refused to tell her why. She said that since therapy commenced she had had several nocturnal dreams which were of a sexual nature and which produced orgasm.

Michaela's Fourth Daydream (Case Ref: O.45):

"I make my way again to the little white cottage, after resting and, as the 4th scroll directs, knock upon the cottage door again and a woman who looks like my mother has come to the doorway. She leads me to the stable where she invites me to select one of the horses. This time I take the golden-brown one.
I mount up and make my way through the forest. I can hear the birds singing. There are lots of dips in the ground and the forest is quite dense in places but thinned out in others. I feel so comfortable on this horse. I have now reached the large oak tree and this time I decide to take the path on its left, leading to a hill. At the top of the hill there are three caves. Leaving my horse outside, I enter the middle one. In the corner I spy the witch. She is old and fat and short, her face is all wrinkled and she looks haggard. Her hair and her clothes are dark, dingy-black and grey. She hasn't seen me. I move towards her holding the chalice out in front of me. I am now right next to her. Suddenly she looks up at me in surprise. Now she is doing something with her hands and is trying to back away from me. I touch her with the chalice and she screams and begins melting. She is just a pool now. I pass this and enter further into the cave. There are five people here all skinny and starving, four men and one woman. They seem surprised to see me. The men are all different but all of them look as if they've been beaten about. One of them is a young man and the other three are middle-aged but they are all dressed so shabbily. How thin the young woman is. She has black hair and is aged about thirty. All of them are tied up in a cage. I am looking around for something to release them. There is a knife and I cut the ropes that bind them. Why are they so alarmed? I try to reassure them. They tell me they just can't believe they're free. I lead them out of the cave where my horse is waiting and we say our farewells as I have to go back to the mountain. I mount up and journey back to the cottage. The only creature I encounter is a single bird. At the cottage I return the horse to the woman who looks like my mother and explain

that I have completed the mission, at which she laughs in disbelief. I tell her that I was able to release some people who were imprisoned.

"There was no witch", the woman says. "That's just an old wives' tale". I say goodbye to her and make my way up the mountain and begin the ascent of the stairs. Once again the old man like my grandfather is there and I tell him what has happened. I have to hand him back the fourth scroll. He is now congratulating me but says I must carry out another mission and gives me the fifth scroll. I hold up my chalice and see that all of it — its two handles are pure gold with a gold-leaf pattern on them and all is encrusted with rubies and diamonds which are sparkling brightly. I return to the foot of the mountain".

Her mother telephoned me before her daughter's next session to say how pleased she was with Michaela's progress. She said that Michaela was much fitter, more confident, putting on weight and eating properly. At the next session Michaela thanked me too.

Beryl's Fourth Daydream (Case Ref: W.154):

"I go back down the stairway, passing the serpent and descend the mountain. I go to the cottage where I am greeted by a woman who is dressed like "Old Father Time". I select a white winged-horse like Pegasus and fly to the cave of the witch. A glow from the mouth of one of several caves indicates that I have found her. I dismount and enter the cave and go down inside it alone. It is hot, uncomfortable. Then I see a green dragon belching forth fire. I have no wish to kill him, so I pour water over him, which puts out his fire whereupon he looks amazed, curls up in a ball and turns away. The glow in the cave has now changed to a predominantly greenish-blue, barely any red in it at all. I feel reluctant to go any further".

Reminding her that in a dream anything is possible, I urge her to continue her descent.

She does so, finally reaching the bottom.

"I can see an old woman in a witch's hat; her face is horrible. She has a hooked nose and a face like a wild animal. She is bent and carries a stick. Suddenly I feel pity for her. There isn't anyone else in the cave. The old witch is unkind to the dragon but really needs him as she has to have *some* company.

"I draw closer to the old woman who begins to cry. She tells me that she will be willing to leave the cave at some time. I give the dragon a cuddle and then leave the cave, rejoining Pegasus. We are walking back to the cottage. A white cockatoo has settled on my shoulder. The wood (forest) is filled with bluebells and I feel wonderfully at peace. I have decided to just sit down and enjoy the peace while Pegasus seems happy to stay by my side and nibble the grass. After a rest we make our way back to the cottage. The old lady there is waiting for us. I tell her that I would like to keep this horse for a while and she has agreed to my request. The monk has now appeared. He holds my hands as he is well pleased. I climb onto the horse's back and we fly up to the top of the mountain and on, up the stairway. On the stairway I have met Sandy, a Labrador with kind eyes who has four or five puppies. I now have both the chalice and the sword. The chalice is like a round bowl with a cross on it; the sword is golden and there is a sheen of light from it. I accept the Fifth Scroll and descend the stairs to the mountain. ... Now I have descended the mountain and returned to the cottage where I have decided to rest in the monk's company before setting off on the next assignment".

Colin's Fourth Daydream (Case Ref: L.70):

" ... I select a grey horse and ride straight to the Sorcerer's cave. The Sorcerer is dressed like Merlin but when I see his face I see the face of my father. He, too, is holding a sword, just like mine! He keeps disappearing in front of me and when he reappears his face keeps changing - a Jester's face, a Knight's face, now animal faces ... and a snake's face. Although I feel threatened I manage to keep calm. I hold my sword in the *en garde* position and feel reasonably confident as I await the inevitable encounter. This turns out to be quite a battle, however, resulting in my piercing Merlin clean through the chest. I now feel very upset as I did not want to harm him. I sadly leave the cave and return to the base of the mountain. I am met by a *Robin Hood-like* person to whom I hand the grey horse. I re-ascend the mountain but on ascending the stairway beyond I am not met by Pure Light but by the figure of a woman dressed in a pure white wedding-gown but her face is black. When I take my sword out to salute her, I see that the blade is dulled and has blood on it".

On the next session, some time later, I encouraged Colin to go through this Daydream again. In his real life situation he began an attempt to live out the dream by improving his relationship with his father although it was proving difficult for him.

"This time I select the black horse which is the swiftest one for I cannot wait to get back into the confrontation with the Sorcerer to put things right. The Sorcerer is wearing a blue cloak and hat, pointed but not too high. The sorcerer surrounds himself with a force field that acts like a magnet and tries to pull my sword away from me. I feel that I must resist this force and yet, I do not wish to harm the Sorcerer, so I try to absorb the power into my own sword. Eventually, I succeed and I am able to leave the Sorcerer's cave without harming him. I sense that the Sorcerer no longer has the power or the intention of harming me. I make my way back to the mountain and ascend the stairway beyond. This time I am met by the Pure Light. I raise my sword, noticing that the blade is now silver, not golden, although the hilt remains golden with diamond studs".

Carl's Fourth Daydream (Case Ref: M.130):

On his descent of the mountain, he again encounters the black dog, which actually bites his hand. After reaching the level ground he is surprised to see an elephant ambling along the road he is travelling. However, this poses no threat to him. Suddenly he sees the witch flying past him on a broomstick.

He reaches the cave of the wizard and on entering it is surprised to find that the inside of the cave is jewelled. He notices a tunnel winding away to the left but the stairs on the right go straight down. He descends these and meets the wizard, a thin, bearded man dressed in a gown and pointed cap. The wizard is not aggressive in manner and is neither afraid nor worried at Carl's presence. Carl feels the need to address the man and feels that he has to ask him for *a key to something.* The wizard hands him a large key and points out the direction he is to take. There he finds a door and the key in his hand enables him to unlock and open this door. Inside is a box on a raised altar. He enters the room and picks up the box and takes it back with him where he returns the key to the wizard but retains the box. He then makes his way back up the steps and out of the cave. The wizard does nothing.

On the return journey to the mountain he experiences a feeling that he is being watched - that others want that box. He begins the ascent of the mountain but rocks fall and some, underfoot, slip. Birds attack him but he is able to fend them off with the straight sword that seems to have enormous power. On the ascent of the stairway he is met by a female, "young, very pretty and clad in a fine long dress". He "instinctively knows that inside the box he is carrying is a ring which he will give the maiden".

His straight sword is glowing with a radiance and brilliance, which makes him feel that his mission has been successfully completed.

Warren's Fourth Daydream (S.164)

"When I descend the mountain it is dark but something is illuminating my way. It is a torch on my left hand side that is suspended in air and guides my way. As I descend further this light moves round to my other side and some distance from me. When I go to the stable near the cottage to collect a horse I discover that a thick granite wall separates me from it. I use my sword to attack the wall and literally cut it down, the sword is so powerful. As the wall falls a dazzling ball of white light with a beautiful horse-like creature is revealed in its midst. To the left of this, in a shaded part, is the wizard. I feel no fear of him as I tower above him and he looks frail and weak and is supporting himself by holding a gnarled stick.

"I decide to return to the mountain but somehow feel a reluctance to turn my back on the wizard so I leave him, walking backwards, until I reach the foot of the mountain. I am able to ascend it with no difficulty and after climbing to the top, make my way up to the fourth stairway again to accept the fifth assignment. My sword is glowing again, perhaps brighter than before . . . "

Stuart's Fourth Daydream (Case Ref: T.68):

His descent was accomplished but not without difficulty and particularly so on the last part of the mountain just before reaching ground level. It necessitated his attaching one end of a rope on an outcrop of rock and tying the other end around his waist and attempting to lower himself down carefully. However, as he descended in this way, he suddenly found himself suspended, *upside down.* Eventually he managed to get to ground level and make his way to the stable where he selected the pure white horse again. When he sat astride the horse, however, he felt that he was "still attached by something round the waist".

He was urged to free himself, cutting the cord if necessary with his sword so that he could proceed with his assignment.

His journey to the wizard's cave accomplished, which he found quite easily, he attempted to gain entry but said: "the entrance is very small and the walls are starting to seal around the horse". He was urged to persist in gaining access, *all things being possible in a dream*, whereupon he discovered that the walls were very thin and he managed to break through them.

He then began a "descent of many steps", saying that they curved round to the left, but the cave itself "seems to be getting smaller and smaller". At the bottom of the steps he described a chamber in the rock "exactly oblong with a curved roof". The Wizard was there. He described the wizard as being "like Merlin with a high and pointed hat, his attitude somewhat aloof". He stood looking at Stuart without making any attempt at communication, then suddenly changed himself into a pterodactyl. After that demonstration, he changed back again into the wizard but extended one arm towards Stuart, which changed into the shape of a cross. Then he began spinning round and round at great speed. As Stuart moved towards him he stopped spinning and Stuart became aware of "the wizard's talon-like nails which he was displaying as he literally scratched at the air around him". Stuart decided that it would be expedient to clip those talons if he were to overcome the wizard but as soon as he cut them off they grew long again. "It seems futile", Stuart remarked in some despair.

"Remember, in a dream anything is possible. What do you think might be the source of the Wizard's power?"

Stuart felt that it was his hat and that if the hat could be removed from the wizard's head, his power would also be removed.

He attempted to slash at the hat with his sword and discovered that cutting from right to left did not help, nor indeed cutting downwards. However, when cutting from left to right, the sword made contact with the hat and it flew from the wizard's head, proceeding to then fly all around the stone room until Stuart managed to catch it.

Feeling certain that he had completed his mission there, Stuart left the room and returned to the mountain. He described the ascent as easier than before and certainly easier than his descent had been. On the stairway beyond he handed the wizard's hat to Jesus and then lifted his sword in salutation. He described it as being "very clean and shining . . . even the hilt . . . "

*　*　*

CHAPTER 9

" ... A large company that is made up of entirely admirable people resembles, in respect to its morality and intelligence, an unwieldy, stupid, and violent animal... "
— Carl G Jung "*Essays on Contemporary Events*".

As we saw in the last two chapters, Desoille's Daydreams 3 and 4 vary, being governed by whether the client who is being guided through them by the therapist is male or female. We will see in chapter 10 that Daydream 6 also follows a different approach according to the sex of the client. However, Daydream 5, at which we will now be looking, follows the same approach regardless of whether the client is a man or a woman and in that respect is similar to Daydreams 1, 2 and 3. Normally, of course, the therapist is working with just one person, his client be that client male or female. Indeed, all six of the Daydreams were designed by Desoille for this *one-to-one* consultation. The necessity for deviating from the norm, arises solely because we are moving from this one-to-one basis to group participation.

When giving a talk on any subject, as far as possible I have tried my very best to involve the group I am addressing in active participation. There is an old Chinese proverb, which says: "If I *hear* it, I forget it; if I *see* it, I remember; if I *do* it, I know". Audiences who are expected to merely sit and listen often end up merely *sitting,* or as a token of respect to the person delivering the talk, doing their best to *look* interested throughout, even though a large part of what has been said went over the heads of most of them after the first few minutes! A situation which can be even worse from the speaker's point of view, of course, if the talk is scheduled to follow on from a meal break; the dreaded "pudding-session" as it is called, for then many of the audience may lose the will to even *look* interested and nod off, some even demonstrating the fact audibly.

Although through many years of using Desoille's Daydream technique in my practice, I had become confident and competent in its application, this had been, of course, on the *one-to-one* basis, the intimate client and therapist situation, which Desoille had intended. It was another matter giving talks on the technique to mixed groups of well over a hundred people, men and women, and expecting audience *participation*. In fact, it was not until I was preparing my notes and planning the first of these public talks, that I suddenly realised I would be forced to confine my talk to Daydreams 1 and 2; both being suitable in their entirety for clients of either sex and therefore possibly suitable for mixed audience participation. Naturally, Desoille's Daydreams have to be worked through in the *order* in which he has set them out; although over my years in Practice I had introduced one or two refinements of my own, based upon observation of the reactions of my own clients, I was in complete accord with Desoille on this order.

Later, working with smaller, mixed classes of half a dozen or so, I found it expedient to divide the students into two separate groups according to their sex.

On the last occasion, instead of my taking each group through all six daydreams personally, I enlisted the help of my wife who took one of the two groups on Daydreams 3, 4 and 6.

The theme of the fifth daydream is an encounter with the fabled dragon that the client (or student) has to search out in the depths of its cave. As Desoille explains: "This [the dragon] is another figure which arises spontaneously in the directed daydream. . .but instead of waiting for (it) to arise, can be evoked by the therapist and used to direct the course of the daydream (in order to) explore the (client's) habitual responses to others. ... In the fable, the dragon hoards a treasure and keeps captive a girl or a boy, who is eventually to be devoured by him, but is rescued by the hero." Desoille points out that this legend has an entirely different meaning within our occidental context than in that of the oriental where the dragon symbolises beneficence. A point worth bearing in mind, especially so perhaps in today's mixed ethnic population.

We will now look at the responses to the fifth daydream of those clients whose progress we have been following:-

Anna's Fifth Daydream (Case Ref: G.118):

"I find myself descending the mountain from the far side. The sides of the mountain here seem very sheer with practically nothing to hold onto and I make my way very slowly. Now I have reached a point where there is a sheer drop. I am trying to gain a foothold on a rock that is rougher than the rest. It is a dark and cloudy day, possibly a storm is brewing. Oh! I have slipped but have managed to grip an outcrop of rock and haul myself back up."

Eventually, after considerable effort, she makes the foot of the mountain and then makes her way round it and across to the cottage with the thatched roof.

"Today there is no-one there so I help myself to supplies including some water and pack them onto the white horse, mount up and set off on my journey across the desert to confront the dragon. The desert is full of sandy dunes and occasional cactus plants, which I make my way around. At last I reach some foothills on the far side of the desert and begin my search for the dragon's cave. I soon find it. It is sloping down into one of the hills and the entrance looks very dark. I enter it alone because the entrance is too small to permit the horse's entry. I proceed along a pathway sloping down into the cave. There seems to be a great deal of water about. I am on a sort of ledge that juts out from one of the walls of the cave. How very dark it is. I can barely see the chalice. There are bends, corners to encounter and I am forced to grope my way round them. I have rounded a corner and now I can see flames a long way off. I make my way towards these flames only to discover that they have gone as I round yet another corner. I sense that I am close to the dragon and I am feeling very afraid. It is so dark and now I can hear the dragon near me although I cannot see it".

At this point she was reminded that in a dream anything can happen and to use the chalice to help her.

"The chalice is giving off a light to help me. Now it's gone out. Now it's come back on again. The dragon does not seem to like this light and is walking away from me. I can see him now. He is huge. He has an enormous mouth and looks like a dinosaur with a very long tail. His body is black and horny; his eyes are bright red. The top of his head is round. His teeth are enormous. He is aware of me and is standing in the water, lashing his tail madly. He is about forty feet away from me but suspects that I am near and is searching for me. I feel that I will have to kill him as he will not permit me to leave his cave alive. He is breathing out flames but I am forcing myself to get closer to him so that I can use the power of the chalice to put out the flames. Although the chalice is empty its power is really great. The dragon's tail thrashes out and pins me to the wall of the cave. I touch his tail with my chalice and this contact makes the dragon's tail whip across to the other side of the cave. I feel that I have put out the dragon's fire permanently. The dragon is now just lying in the water, no longer any threat to me. I am making my way back to where I left the white horse but the ledge is far more slippery as the walls are wet where the dragon thrashed about. Eventually I manage to reach the white horse and climb upon his back. I make my way back towards the mountain, passing lots of cactus bushes, more than before. I return the white horse to its stable and without him begin the ascent of the mountain. I am able to ascend it without too much difficulty although it is still cloudy and stormy conditions prevail which do not seem to bother me unduly. When I reach the top of the mountain I see the shaft of golden light and eagerly ascend it. I am pleased to see God's kindly eyes, bushy white eyebrows and long white hair. He is dressed in a gold robe. I hand him the fifth scroll and accept from him the sixth one. Once again I am given the choice of where to rest before setting off on the sixth assignment. I decide once more to rest at the top of the mountain. I hold up the chalice in salutation. It is now golden, shining, its ends are more pointed in shape and the inside is of shining silver. The chalice is dish-shaped, flat at the base and its appearance is more stream-lined than before."

Barbara's Fifth Daydream (Case Ref: C.133):

"This time I select a dappled-grey cart-horse and begin to cross a desert to reach the dragon when I suddenly find that my horse is sinking into the sand and I am forced to dismount and walk with him, making slow progress. Eventually the sand becomes firmer underfoot and much flatter (no dunes). The cave of the dragon is situated in a rocky peak. I enter the cave after tethering the horse outside. The floor of the cave descends and suddenly I come face to face with the dragon, which actually resembles a Chinese Dragon with brightly coloured striped face. Its eyes are huge and its mouth full of teeth that make it have the appearance of a silly smile. Its expression is bemused and unintelligent. It begins dancing as if in a carnival. This fills me with indecision for I do not know how to deal with it; finally in desperation, I fling my cup at it. As the cup strikes it on the head it rapidly diminishes in size until it becomes but a mask left upon the ground. I return to the mountain and ascend the stairway and report what has happened to the Higher Being who is jubilant. However, he is asking me for my cup and I realise with horror that I have left it in the dragon's cave! The Higher Being is annoyed about that and orders me to go back to retrieve it. I am forced to retrace my steps but am relieved to find the cup on the floor of the cave where it had fallen. I retrieve it and journey back to the mountain once again, ascend it and present the cup to the Higher Being. Although breathless through my exertions I feel elated; the cup is shining more brightly than ever."

Eleanor's Fifth Daydream (Case Ref: F.19):

"Once again I make my way from the foot of the mountain to the thatched cottage by a stream where I shall select a horse for my journey to find the dragon. This time I select the magical horse, a mauve-black horse with flecks of white in its mane and a star in its forehead. Facing me is a desert that is stony, studded with cacti, bristly bushes are blowing about. As I cross this desert I encounter mice and a snake but they constitute no threat. It is dry and there are vultures circling high up in the sky. A blazing, relentless sun beats down upon me. Ahead are the mountains that resemble cones.

"There is the cave of the dragon, littered with large bones. There seem to be many entrances but I see the dragon's one. Inside the floor of the cave slopes downward and there are three human sculls in the mouth of the cave and there is a foul stench assailing my nostrils. I am dismounting from my horse and proceeding on foot. I feel that there are advantages in going it alone. I am dressed like the fool in the tarot— two shades of green — more of a masculine figure. Although the cave is dark I have *the light from the chalice.* I smell fire. There are two fluted columns supporting a rampart with stone dragons at the top. The light from the Chalice throws up large macabre shadows against the walls accentuating the images of the stone dragons. Now there is a bend in the tunnel and as I round it there is a great roaring and flames and smoke. The dragon has only one head and is fat. It has a long nose, red evil eyes, very large teeth and a whip-like tail with a spike on the end. He is about the size of a small horse. He is aware of my presence and produces more fire. There is a pathetic stance about him in spite of his malevolent face. The power of the Chalice keeps him at bay. The solution is to kill him and as I think this a sword materialises in my left hand; I am holding the Chalice in my right. The sword is of flaming gold.

"He seems to be unable to attack very well. I think that his ferocious appearance and his noise, his showiness, has kept people at bay. I plunge the sword into his neck; the blood is of a watery-purple viscous sap that exudes from him. The fire diminishes and the dragon collapses in a heap. The body shrinks as the fluid leaks out from his wound. He is dead.

"I am returning to the cave mouth and remounting the horse. We gallop back. The desert feels cooler and there are more cacti and animals than before. On the horizon there is a rain cloud. Now rain begins to fall on the desert and as if by magic under the cloud, grass and trees begin to grow. The vegetation stretches right across the desert and there are now many creatures. A rainbow has appeared.

"I return the horse and ascend the mountain and the stairway beyond where I meet the figure of the kindly being with his long lined face, good nose. How quiet he is and how beautiful his face. His robes are of crimson and gold. I hand him the scroll containing the result of my encounter with the dragon. He accepts it and is handing me the sixth scroll, perhaps my final mission. The Chalice is silvery-gold and is still pouring out the everlasting force. The stem is encrusted with many precious jewels of many coloured hues. I decide this time to rest on the peak of the mountain before embarking on the sixth mission."

Anita's Fifth Daydream (Case Ref: G.93):

"I took the brown horse and rode across the desert towards six distant caves. I encountered no difficulties on my journey. When I reached the six caves I selected the fourth one from the left where I knew the dragon to be. Leaving the brown horse outside I entered the cave on foot. The dragon was very large, of a greenish colour and belching smoke and flames from its nostrils. I went to the top of a staircase, which had stone steps, *to rise above it.* I held the vessel up and a beam of light shone through it onto the dragon, which began to shrink. It continued to shrink until it was about half its former size. I threw some precious stones from my vessel towards it in the hope that it would eat them but it didn't. I then made a necklace of more of the stones and flung the loop over the dragon's head. The dragon shrunk until eventually it disappeared altogether; the necklace remained on the floor. I reluctantly gathered up the stones and put them in a bag (I wanted them separate from the unsoiled ones in the vessel). I made my way back without incident, returned the horse, climbed the mountain and then the stairway. This time the Angelic Being had a halo round his head (for some reason I was reminded of my grandmother) and white hair of even length. The Angel was well pleased with me and kept the stones that had been soiled. The vessel had a greenish-white hue. I accepted the scroll from the Heavenly Body for my final assignment but decided to rest at a point half way down the mountain before undertaking the mission."

Rita's Fifth Daydream (Case Ref: M.37):

"The mountain is now covered in green grass and my descent is easy. I make my way swiftly to the cottage and select a chestnut horse that is ready saddled. I ride round the mountain and see a desert stretching before me. I begin the journey across it; the terrain is flat and firm beneath the horse's feet. A strong wind begins to blow and I see a sandstorm sweeping across the desert towards me. I dismount and begin leading the horse, my head bent down to avoid the stinging sand. Then quite suddenly the storm is past my side and the sun is out. there are a few brightly coloured flowers, mainly reds and yellows, but no other signs of life. Near the foothills at the far side of the desert there appear burnt trees, possibly caused by the dragon breathing his fire. The dragon is at the bottom of the hill — he is quite fiery — he is waiting for something. He is not so big, perhaps smaller than a room. He sees me, turns and makes a noise. I hold up the chalice whereupon the dragon puts up his head and disappears inside himself, turning into a golden dragon instead of a green one and sprouting large wings. He is powerful but his power is generally generated by another. He was under some sort of spell to lay waste to things about him but he has been rescued from outside, not within. He has been set free. Feeling my mission has been accomplished, I make my way back across the desert; the flowers and the storm are there still. The storm is *Tibetan* - currents of air are taking on entities but I just have to go through it. This time, however, as I saw the storm approaching, I am prepared and cover myself and my horse's eyes. At last I am out of the storm and once again the mountain is in sight. A girl is running towards us and as she draws level with us says. "Oh! You've done it!" and then disappears. She was dressed as a peasant. Now I am at the cottage and saying goodbye to the horse. I ascend the mountain very much aware of the gritty feel of sand in my clothes, which is making movement uncomfortable. I have decided to stop climbing and undress and shake the sand from all my clothes. When I have done this, I put my clothes back on and resume climbing. I reach the peak without mishap and ascend the golden stairway that veers round to the right. This time I climb much higher than usual. It is dark and I am forced to cross an even darker space; it is like walking on a cloud with the stars underneath me.

"A man with grey, curly hair, bald centre, smooth-shaven, tall, strong with an incredibly gentle face meets me. He is wearing a brown robe and is priest-like, almost pope-like. He takes the fifth scroll from me and thanks me. He is now handing me the sixth and final scroll. I raise the chalice in salutation and it suddenly becomes like a huge butterfly enveloping the chalice. The chalice is bathed in clear blue light. I decide that I will not rest but will undertake the final mission at once..."

Sylvia's Fifth Daydream (Case Ref: M.164):

"In this mission I have selected a brown horse on which I cross the desert. The sun is hot but not unpleasant. The desert is golden and flat with the odd sand dune and cactus here and around. I feel as if I shall never find the hole where the dragon is. There are strings of holes in the rock-face ahead and he could be in any of them. I choose the biggest one and ride towards it. The dragon comes out, roars and then goes back in. My feeling towards this dragon is that it isn't going to harm me. In fact, he seems to be totally indifferent to me - almost ignoring me. However, I feel that it would not be wise to provoke him as if he wished he could destroy me. As in the episode with the Sorcerer I feel that the decision was his and that nothing I could do, chalice or not, could change this. I pour some liquid from the chalice on its two front feet and am aware that although this would present him with difficulties, I still felt I could not *disarm* him. It is as if I keep quiet I could be OK; to do battle with him seems foolish.

"He is sleeping so I pour some of the liquid from the chalice over his tail. At first the tail disappears but then two tails appear. I don't want to be responsible for its destruction so I leave the dragon in its cave and journey back to the mountain, leading the horse. I return it to the man in charge of the stables and climb the mountain and then the stairs beyond. As I look up, I see the monk but the dragon is between him and me. Now the monk seems to have the face of the dragon. As I hold up the chalice the monk's face returns to normal but he is smiling. I accept the final scroll from him. The chalice is now shining more brightly. I descend the mountain and rest there awhile".

Michaela's Fifth Daydream (Case Ref: O.45):

"At the cottage I select the brown race-horse and set off across the desert. There is a snake slithering across the sand. It is a greenish-grey colour. There is sand for miles and the desert is flat although I can see green hills in the distance. After a while I reach some rocky ground and see ahead of me three caves. I enter the one on the left and its entrance is big so I can remain on horseback. There is nothing here but darkness. I enter the middle cave and once again there is nothing but darkness. I am now inside the third cave. A dragon is in the far corner. It is huge and scaly; greyish-green in colour with large fish-like scales down its middle. Its tail is thick and long to the tip, which is sharp. It has large red eyes and short pointed ears. Its feet are massive with four claws on each foot. It is staring at the ground. I climb off my horse and quietly creep towards the dragon, holding the chalice in front of me. It has seen me and its red eyes are glowing in the dark. I touch it with my chalice. *Flash-bang*; it disappears. Once again I explore the cave and see drawings on the walls, foreign writing and symbols. I leave the cave, mount up and ride back across the desert. It is very hot. My horse is travelling at a comfortable pace. It is getting so hot as the sun blazes down on the sand. There, just ahead, is my mountain. I am glad to see it.

"I return the horse to its stable and begin the ascent. I slip but manage to recover myself. Now I am at the top and once again climb the stairs where I am again met by my grandfather figure. Again he is well pleased with me and hands me the final scroll. My chalice is glowing and I see clearly its golden leaf pattern and glowing diamonds and rubies. I descend to the shack at the foot of the mountains and rest awhile".

Beryl's Fifth Daydream (Case Ref: W.154):

"I select a white horse, *Purity*, and set off on my journey across the desert. Nothing untoward happens on my journey and finally ahead of me I see a cave, the floor of which is sloping downwards. I have not descended very far when I encounter the dragon that is just like the dragons in the fables. The dragon seems very angry at my intrusion, blowing out fire. It is massive, greenish, scaly, with lots of arms and has a very long pointed nose. Its eyes are closed and taking advantage of this, I get closer to it ...

"...but I have decided to sit and watch it. The dragon is now trying to intimidate me by blowing smoke and fire and making a lot of noise. I rise to my feet but he does not frighten me unduly and I am able to stand firm. I am wondering why it had burned up the earth around to create a barren desert. Eventually the dragon becomes exhausted and ceases to produce any fire and flops down on a rock. It is asking me why I am not frightened like everyone else.

I reply that I just am not! Whereupon the dragon tells me that certain things are expected of a dragon, which is why he had to behave like one. He explains that the outcome of all this had resulted in his having no friends since everyone was frightened of him. I tell him that I quite like him, that really he is quite nice. I explain to him that I will make friends if he ceases to behave badly. The dragon seems stunned by this and I feel that he does not believe me. I decide to prove it. I tell him that I shall remain with him a few days.

"I have remained with him a few days, displaying him the beauty he should not destroy. For his part he accepted the terms and behaved well. I enjoy this new attitude and when I take my leave of him I know that he has been tamed. An Arab on a black horse is waiting for me and asks me to "go the other way with him". I am riding through the desert with him where the terrain is sandy and flat. We reach an oasis where we pitch a tent. There are children about but no sign of any other men and women. We sit and talk together about the place where he lives and he tells me that he would like me to stay. I have doubts about staying and decide to return to the cottage and the mountain. I leave him and set off alone, crossing the desert and finally reaching the cottage. I return the white horse and then begin the ascent of the mountain. On the mountain I meet a pleasant-looking man with dark, curly hair; he is standing on a ledge as if he knew that I would come back. I continue climbing but when I reach the peak, the Arab is standing there. I feel tempted to stop but finally I overcome the temptation and I pass him by and begin climbing the stairway ... where I meet Christ ... the real living spiritual Christ who is waiting for me with His arms outstretched. I give Him my Chalice. He accepts the Chalice and the scroll from me and leaves the sixth scroll for me in a golden cup with a lid, adorned by a crown, on top. It is decorated too. I meet the Arab on the mountain but the other man is also waiting and I feel that I have to choose between them. I *know* that I cannot go with the other man and that he will be hurt; the Arab touches me warmly, then he and I ascend the stairway together and look down as if it were the last time I will see that part of myself. We mount two horses and ride together through the clouds, he on a black horse, me on a white one. I feel exhilarated by the freedom and go back with him to his tent in the oasis. Although the people there are poor, they are kind and I want to stay there".

She interpreted this as wanting the man of her dreams but that she could only do it in the dream state.

Colin's Fifth Daydream (Case Ref: L.70):

"... I select the brown horse and begin my journey across the desert. It is totally barren and the air is hot and has sand blowing in it. I do not like this area and believe that it poses some threat. After journeying for some time I reach the other side of the desert where I believe the dragon is to be found. I realise that my horse is tired and dry so I give it some of the water from my canister. The daylight is beginning to fade so I decide to rest overnight before tackling the dragon. The next morning I see a monk carrying a bundle of wood and he tells me where the dragon can be found, in a cave nearby. When I enter this cave I discover that the dragon is in the process of devouring someone. I go right up to the dragon who tells me that he does not cause trouble but some of the people do. The dragon breathes no fire on me nor makes any attempt to harm me. I leave the dragon and go into the village where I make enquiries of the villagers; some like the dragon, some don't; those who do seem to be trustworthy and those who don't, untrustworthy. I go back to the dragon who is sad and tells me that the person he devoured tried to kill him first and that it was people like him who damaged the land and tried to put the blame on him, the dragon. The dragon is weeping and I tell him that I believe him.

"Those of the villagers who said that they disliked the dragon now begin to attack it and me but the sword creates a space which keeps them apart from us. Then, one by one, they admit that they are wrong and will now accept the dragon and live in peace. I return to the cottage and hand back the horse and then ascend the mountain and the stairway beyond where, on the 13th stair I meet the Light. I feel tired as my encounter on this assignment was not easy. When I raise my sword in salutation to the Light I notice that although it is bright, its blade now is bronze, not gold and the handle, although patterned as before, seems darker".

Carl's Fifth Daydream (Case Ref: M.130):

On his descent of the mountain this time, he is confronted by a 6' high barbed wire fence. He manages to scale this, not without difficulty, and descends the opposite side of the mountain and then sets off across the desert. The sands beneath his feet he describes as being slippery but with difficulty crosses them to reach a cool oasis where he is able to rest. He describes the oasis as being quite unoccupied except for himself. Blackbirds are swooping about between the oasis and the mountain. After resting, he leaves the oasis, his haven as he describes it, and sets out once more. He is surprised to find an elephant preceding him! At last he finds the dragon's cave, high in the hills but unmistakable because "spurts of flame are issuing from it". He climbs the incline, which he describes as "a rocky access, not a proper pathway", realising that he has not formulated any proper plan. He realises that he should formulate a purposeful plan before entering the dragon's cave. The conclusion he reaches is that he will make a disturbance; an impact with the intention of drawing the dragon out of the cave. This he proceeds to do and the dragon emerges from the entrance of the cave. He describes the dragon as "green, smelly, venomous and fierce". He decides to use the curved sword and thrusts at its eyes. However, the dragon has sharp eyesight and manages to avoid the curved sword so Carl uses the straight sword instead and goes for the dragon's throat. This time he is successful and the dragon cannot evade the swift thrust.

Having overcome the dragon, he decides to explore the cave and finds that it is full of jewels. He wants these so begins filling a sack, which he finds nearby. He keeps adding more jewels and then discovers that the sack has become very heavy. The bones of the dragon's victims are also in the cave. He leaves the cave and sets off on the journey back to the mountain but the going is hard because of the weight of the sack of jewels and he is relieved to find rest at the oasis. Again, he is alone and enjoys the rest and the quiet moments alone. Eventually he sets off again and reaches the mountain. It is more difficult to climb because of the sack of jewels but he persists in carrying the heavy sack. He finds that it is very difficult climbing over the barbed wire fence and cuts his arms, his forearms in the process. Now he is at the top of the mountain and climbing the shaft of light where he meets the wise old man and the girl, the young girl. He hands over the sack of jewels to the old man "as proof of his victory over the dragon". As he does so the thought goes through his head that the jewels could bring material security but somehow this seems less important than handing them over to the old man.

Warren's Fifth Daydream (Case Ref: S.164):

"The path down the mountain seems steeper. ... Once more I select the horse with the white nose and set off to face the dragon. My route lies through a desert that has soft, loose sand making the going hard. By the time I reach the hills at the edge of the desert it is beginning to get dark and suddenly the witch appears on my left hand side. As I enter the hills, however, the figure of the witch gets smaller. Suddenly, "I" am out of my body and floating above both the horse and the witch so I grasp hold of the horse's mane. The shell of myself is standing beside the witch but the real me *is going away from her*".

"Go back!"

"I am being ordered back. Again, one aspect of myself is mounting the horse but I am leaving another shell behind. Now I am surrounded by Light and I am able to go right through the shell and remount the horse. The witch is getting smaller and smaller and although the background is darkened I AM IN THE LIGHT. The sun is now rising above the hills and the dragon appears - it is gigantic, dwarfing the hills. It is green and scaly with fire coming from its mouth. I am wearing a black cloak and hat. I slash the dragon broadside on with my sword and although this makes it keel over, it now has the sword in its mouth. I pull the sword free and wipe it clean. I am walking away from the dragon now which still has an eye on me but it no longer poses any threat and is becoming smaller and smaller. I am moving towards the hills that in contrast to the dragon are getting larger. I am still bathed in a pool of light. The witch is still following me and pointing her stick at me angrily and I don't seem to be getting anywhere. So, I hold up my sword like a cross and face the witch whereupon she becomes calm and shrinks. I decide to return to the mountain and set out once more across the desert that now has vegetation springing up all around.

" I have completed my journey and have returned the horse to its stable. I cannot wait to reascend the mountain".

He climbs it with ease, fairly "zipping" up its side and the stairway beyond, to the fifth stair.

Stuart's Fifth Daydream (Case Ref: T.68):

The descent of the mountain is undertaken without too much difficulty but finds it very difficult to cross the desert, eventually calling on Higher forces to help him. (Jesus, the Christ). Eventually reaches the cave of the dragon but when he tries to enter it a strong wind blows him back. The force tumbles him about outside the cave entrance and then the dragon emerges. Stuart struggles to his feet and then draws his sword and prepares to do battle with the dragon. The dragon lashes out at him with its long tail, which is barbed at the end. Stuart, with a sweep of his sword, cuts off the tail that still wriggles about. He slashes at the body of the dragon and actually cuts it in half, whereupon his father and his mother emerge. He has liberated them. His father pats him on the back and Stuart feels that he has earned his father's praises. The dragon meanwhile has transferred its energy to its tail and both parents now encourage him in his fight with it. In spite of everything he feels that each of his parents, within their limitations, do wish to see him succeed. As he strikes at it, the dragon's tail shrinks to half its former size and no longer constitutes as much of a threat as before. Stuart crosses the desert with his parents and then ascends the mountain alone without difficulties. On the stairway beyond, he hands over the fifth scroll to Jesus, reluctantly. He explains that he had been unable to slay the dragon. Jesus looks at him with kindly eyes and Stuart feels that although he had not achieved a complete victory by slaying the dragon, he has somehow achieved an *emotional* victory, which is difficult to rationalise on an analytical level.

*   *   *

CHAPTER 10

When our true selves are all released, set free
From all the cares and woes of this, our life,
When pain can no more pierce us with her knife,
Or passion shake us on her soundless sea.
- D. Olamano (*Oppertetrix*)

The sixth and final of Desoille's Directed Daydreams is that associated with *the Sleeping Beauty,* a story of which most of us will be familiar. Like Daydreams 3 and 4, it is conducted differently for men and women. Incidentally, it has been my practice *usually* to have conducted it differently with groups of students than in the *therapy* situation. In the client situation, *before* he or she is guided through the final daydream, in the case of the male client, he is first asked to recall any memory, pleasant or unpleasant, of an experience with his mother, while the female client is asked to evoke a memory of any incident involving her father. Having first done this, the client only then is asked to embark upon the sixth daydream. For the male client, his mission is to search for the castle of the Sleeping Beauty, enter it and awaken her from sleep. For the female client, she is asked to imagine that she *is* the Sleeping Beauty.

Occasionally, I have encountered clients of either sex who are not familiar with the Sleeping Beauty story and it is then necessary, briefly, to relate the story to them before they can be guided through its experience.

The following is an account of the sixth daydream related by ***Marie,*** who is a teacher aged 33, married with two children. This client, French by birth and married to an Englishman, knew of Robert Desoille's Psychotherapeutics and had consulted me because she was suffering from what had been diagnosed as "acute anxiety state" and which the orthodox medical approach had failed to assist her in overcoming. During our therapy sessions, she was, of course, taken through all six of the daydreams but I did not select her case to illustrate the first five simply because her responses with these, although very useful from the analysis and therapy point of view, nevertheless followed a fairly average, almost mundane, pattern. However, those who are familiar with the stories of *The Sleeping Beauty* and *Beauty and the Beast,* will recognise that Marie seems to have confused the two in her own mind; and it is because of this fact and its connection with the underlying problem which she had suffered and the effectiveness of *her sixth* daydream in overcoming and resolving it, that I have chosen to include it here; particularly as her experience was instrumental in my introducing some refinement to Desoille's Sixth Daydream in subsequent therapy sessions with clients who appeared to have a similar underlying problem.

I will begin Marie's account by explaining that at the end of the fifth daydream she went back up the mountain and climbed the stairway beyond, where she met, as on her previous four daydreams, "the Superior Being" and described her chalice as being "now mostly tarnished apart from a triangular, bright-yellow part at the top left handle".

Marie (Case Ref: C.132):

"With the scroll detailing the final assignment and the chalice in my hands, I went back down (the mountain) and read the instructions which required me to go to a castle. To get there I was required to go through a forest, which I proceeded to do on horseback. At a large oak tree the path divided in two and at first I started off along the left path but subsequently decided to take the right one instead. By following this I finally came onto another path leading to a drawbridge over a moat. The drawbridge was open. I entered a courtyard and went into the castle through the left-hand side door, the central door having been permanently blocked off. I went up some steps, turned right along a corridor and down some more steps to find myself in the entrance hall, on the other side of the central door.

"I went up the grand staircase that divided at the first landing into two smaller flights of stairs, one on each side. I went up the left one and opened the first door on the left.

"Inside was a piano, some clothes left lying on a stand. The room was currently inhabited although there was noone there at the time. To its left seemed to be the start of a corridor leading to a courtyard from which I could see the light. Along that corridor, (were) some brooms and stainless steel buckets. I shut the door and proceeded to the second door. In there were mostly household tools: brooms, mops, a bucket and cloths. The walls were bare and greyish. Some housework pinafores were hanging at the back of the door. I closed the door again and then proceeded back to the top of the stairs to start at the first bedroom on the right.

"I opened its door. The room had been used as a study with bookshelves on each side, a window at the back and in front of the window, a writing desk. Yet a spider web was spread across the room, with a huge black furry spider on the web. I did not step into the room as I hate spiders but proceeded to kill it, since I knew that I would have to tackle a beast in the turret and did not want this spider to come to the beast's rescue. I used the chalice, which sprayed red paint-like spray onto the creature, which immediately shrunk and was sucked into the chalice where it vanished.

"I closed the door and proceeded to the second room which had no back wall but opened onto a huge green and yellow garden. On the right, stretched a patch of yellow (flowers) which I now associated with a garden I knew; it was lovely to know the aperture into the garden was there! I closed the door again and opened the fourth door. I cannot remember opening a third... oh, yes! It was a cupboard under some stairs with more household equipment and a window behind the stairs. Then I opened the fourth door and could see in my mind the Beast on the turret. There, facing this window, stood a ghost-like figure in a dirty white robe with a hood on it. Suddenly the beast turned and faced me with its slimy skeleton face. Its fingers were long and sharp. I could feel my neck freeze and a cold wave overwhelming my body. I could no longer move, only my eyelids. I wanted to stop breathing to make him believe I was not alive. I wanted to stop looking and keeping my eyes open as I felt they revealed what I was and made me vulnerable.

"Yet, I could not close them. The Ghost grasped hold of me and the feel of its arms and hands on my arms was repellent to me. It carried me to an adjacent room and threw me onto its bed, and slavering, told me he wanted to make me his bride. At the time this thought terrified me for I was sure that he was going to kill me during the marriage ceremony but seen from now, maybe I should have been pleased as this would indicate I had a way to his heart; a way to influence him and maybe could resume life after a fashion.

"He then tore the sleeve of my left arm from the shoulder down and clutched both his hands round my neck as if to fasten me to the bed and show me that I was in his power, that he was the all-powerful and that I would in no way escape his brutality. His hands were now human and dirty black. I tried to absent myself in spirit knowing there was nothing I could do but wait until he was through with this fit. I had to keep my eyes open for it would have infuriated him otherwise, as if he was exercising his power over somebody who was not there. I felt I had turned into ice and all my body was frozen, apart from my head, which remained able to think. He then said he had to go and get something and would be back. I was sure that he was going to get a weapon to kill me.

"I stayed there all day, through the dark night when I *see* this horrible single eye, the glare of which I could not stand without damaging myself inside, staring at me from outside the window. It was the stare of someone abnormal, someone who could not be reasoned with and was totally horrific, bestial.

"I was going through mental torture and felt that I must have been quite evil to have to withstand this glare which I felt was awaiting me in hell when the day of reckoning would come. At last it was dawn and I could hear soldiers and a metallic noise underneath but too far to communicate. I knew this would have been useless anyway.

"There was a white sheet under me. Looking back on it, I think I must have been like a dead person displayed on the deathbed and the room was my shrine. I was alone with my fears and my conscience.

"On the third day, I heard the noise of bells round the necks of the cows on the Alps, an area I like a lot; the cockerel sang. My fear was now giving way to anger and decided that I had nothing to lose; it could not get worse. I was determined to shake off my passivity and take the offensive and kill myself. I could see myself as being of a yellow colour now the positive energy was filling my body. I felt as though I could move my head too. I was prepared to face up to the beast no matter what the risks and kill it, even if I was going to die in the process.

"When I heard some metallic sounding footsteps climbing the wooden stairs, I panicked a little; it was the beast, I felt sure and when I heard the door open I felt that I was doomed. Then I was aware of a shape bending over my body and felt the warmth of a kiss on my lips. I no longer felt afraid, I had a feeling it was my mother for a moment. Yet, when I opened my eyes, I woke up in a bright hospital room, talking to my surgeon.

"He was smiling, joking, still wearing the green hat and the white gown from the operation. I was so happy to see him, part of the outside world, welcoming me to freedom. I was safe - away from the horrible room in the turret that reminded me of my bedroom at home.

"I was still weak but happy, peaceful and sure that I would be able to make it to a normal life ..."

We will now resume our examination of the accounts of the Sixth and final Daydreams given by the other clients whose progress we have been following.

Anna's Sixth Daydream (Case Ref. G.118):

"I select the grey horse at the cottage although there is no-one there when I arrive. I journey through the forest, at the far side of which is the castle surrounded by a moat. The castle is big, grey-black in colour and has four towers. The drawbridge is down and I enter the courtyard beyond where I leave my horse and proceed on foot through the oak doorway into the hall beyond. At the top of the stairway leading from the hall is a large landing with six doors leading off. The first room (on the left) is empty. The second, a larger room than the first, contains a table and four chairs and another chair in the corner. The third room is very small and contains many small boxes which, after opening a few and finding to be empty, I assume are all empty. The fourth room is also very small and completely empty. The fifth contains nothing but a large box and I decide to open it. Its hinged lid is extremely heavy but I manage to open it and am horrified to see that it contains something slimy, green and horrible and which begins to get bigger and I notice that it is covered in red spots - ugh! it is slimy, repulsive ... grotesque. It is just beyond description".

I insist that she describes it as fully as possible.

"It is sort of like liquid which can take on any shape and is now a heaving, moving mass. It is still in the box so I close the lid down quickly and leave the room. In the sixth room, also empty, there are fourteen cupboards lining one of the walls". *Are you going to open them?* She proceeds to do so. The first, she tells me, contains nothing but old bottles. The second, third, fourth, fifth, sixth, seventh, eighth and ninth cupboards are all empty. The tenth, however, is *not* empty.

What is there?

"There is a creature inside it. It looks like a man but bigger and not exactly a human form - very ugly, grotesque, fat featured and no eyebrows, filthy long black hair and the most horrible eyes like saucers. It must be about eight or nine feet tall. It is standing there just looking at me so I try to shut the door but I have the chalice in my left hand and this creature, a male, is far stronger than I am. He pushes the door open again and grips hold of my wrists with one of his huge and powerful hands. Oh! the chalice has fallen to the floor. He tells me that he has taken over my castle but that I am to stay here with him. He hands me a bottle and tells me to drink from it and that if I do so I shall not be harmed but if I refuse I shall be punished. I take a sip and immediately fall into a kind of sleep. At least, my body becomes limp but I can still see and hear him. He lifts me up and carries me to the second room containing the table and chairs. In a far corner, out of sight of the door, is a bed and he puts my body down on the bed. I can see through a window a tree and the sky beyond which is overcast. The creature tells me that I shall remain here as his prisoner and that no-one can possibly rescue me. He leaves the room and I am laying here unable to move, waiting for his return and whatever fate he has in mind for me. After some while I hear a noise and I am very frightened because the room seems to be quite dark. I panic as I sense that someone is in the room but I cannot move my head. Suddenly I feel a kiss and then, how wonderful, I am able to move again. It is not the creature who has released me ... the person who is there is my old family doctor."

This obviously surprised her. I ask her if she wishes him to accompany her on her return to the mountain and beyond, to report what has happened.

"I recover my chalice and thank my family doctor. He does not want to accompany me when I explain to him that I must return to the mountain and beyond to report what has happened. I say good-bye to him and remount the grey horse in the courtyard and make my way back to the cottage where I return the horse and then make my way to the mountain, which I ascend quite easily, safely reaching the golden stairway beyond. I ascend this and meet God on the stairway coming down to me. He is dressed in gold and his eyes are so kind as He listens to my account of what has happened. He now accepts the sixth scroll from me and I hold up my chalice which is of a brilliant yellow-gold, it is flat-bottomed, boat shaped and inside it is gleaming purest white, like God's hair and beard."

Accept the seventh scroll which He is handing you and the contents of which will be explained to you.

Later I explain to her that the one further mission is the ***ongoing*** *one of* ***her life.***

Barbara's Sixth Daydream (Case Ref: C.133):

"This time I select a brown race-horse. The forest is pretty and I am able to appreciate its appeal even though nervous about my mission. The castle is in the centre of a clearing and has a moat. It looks eerie, like Dracula's castle and I can sense evil. I cross the drawbridge and enter the castle. Inside, the floor is wooden and uncarpeted; the doors are of dark oak. All is still, apart from the ticking of a grandfather clock. I ascend the staircase to the floor above where there are six doors."

I ask her to open them one by one to see what is beyond.

She tells me that the first two are bedrooms but they are unoccupied. She then opens the third door and is immediately confronted by *Dracula.*

"He is a horrifying creature!"

Describe him!

"He is wearing a black cloak. He has greasy sleeked-down hair, protruding fangs for teeth. His eyes are dark and evil with pink around the eyelids. He seizes hold of me and I am paralysed with fear and my cup falls to the floor. He ties me to a wooden four-poster bed so that I am unable to move. I am frightened, terrified".

I remind her that anything can happen in a dream, can she use her cup?

She says that it is on the floor, a wooden floor. Even the walls are wood-panelled.

"I can see the sky through the chink in the heavy curtains. Dracula leaves me and the room becomes dark as night falls. I see the moon, not a full one but somehow quite comforting. All night I lay there, dozing at times, until dawn. Still Dracula does not return. All through the day noone comes to the room and daylight is replaced by night once more. I am convinced that Dracula intends to make me one of "them". I worry about this all night and at daybreak still noone has visited me. I can see fluffy clouds in the blue sky. I begin to worry about the cup on the floor in case Dracula returns and picks it up. All day I am alone then once more night falls; I am feeling thirsty and hungry, then weak and frightened. I worry now — *will I ever see my family again?* Silvery moonbeams play on the cup, which I can see quite clearly as it is now bigger. I begin to wish something would happen, even a return of the vampire and death would be better than just lying here. I cannot see the door but hear the sound like a cloak rustling and then I'm aware of someone bending over me and kissing me on my mouth. I open my eyes to find someone similar-looking to my husband by the bed. He smiles and releases me, explaining that the castle is really his.

"My mission is over and I tell him that I must return to the mountain to report what has happened, to the Higher Being. My husband accompanies me; we ascend the mountain and the stairway together. The Higher Being is very quiet, displaying no emotion but I feel confident in him. The cup is now much larger, silver and standing upon a rostrum where it is shining and bright. Yet in spite of its size it is much lighter. I feel jubilant."

Eleanor's Sixth Daydream (Case Ref: F.19):

"This time I have selected the white horse and find myself journeying through a long, deep forest, thick with undergrowth. Although the castle is a few days journey the white horse is Pegasus and can make the journey swiftly. Ahead a clearing looms up and I can see the castle. It is very beautiful and situated high on a rocky outcrop and the sun is glinting upon its windows. Pegasus has set me down outside so I cross the drawbridge and enter a courtyard. Opposite me is the main entrance to the building. I enter the door to find myself on a balcony above a great hall. At first I saw two doors but it now seems there are an infinite number of doors beyond these. Gripping the Chalice in my left hand, I open the first door with my right. Beyond is a sumptuous room with tapestries and golden tassels and windows that are long with leaded panes but I have the impression of great wealth, which has been ransacked and the room is now empty. I try the second room but the door handle is stiff and I am setting the Chalice down so that I have both hands free to turn the handle. Slowly the door opens with much creaking and squeaking. The room is dark and dusty and I need the Chalice to illuminate this room. I sense a horror, a terror, a ghostly feeling. Everything is covered in dust-sheets —big chairs, table all lumpy and grim and ... horror. There is an unearthly feeling. I must hold the Chalice in this place of negation. Ah ... it is the imprint of the beast filling the room with horror. The beast is a "no-form" his "*horribleness*" is that he is not warm-blooded, not material, like a black hole. He is more than death, he is beyond blackness, terrible, a negation of life. The Chalice is *part of me.* I feel that I am challenging him with LIFE, daring him to overcome. To overcome the beast means total giving. I feel myself lifted up and placed upon a couch. The side of this *chaise longue* is of black satin piped in gold. It is very black, dark, like a cave with rocky strong ceiling. Although very dark there is a light source. Time is irrelevant. The beast has taken on a malevolent form - the devil. He is covered in a cloak and a mask.

"There seems to be a lift in the oppressive quality; it *is* lighter. The bad smell has gone. I can now see a great candelabra carved in metal, a grand piano. No window. I am aware of the passing of time ... one day and night, the next day and night and now into the third. I do not like this waiting state and am impatient for something to happen. Ah ... a door is opening. I feel less sanguine.

"The person I see is no longer in a cloak and mask. I have unmasked him and he is young, masculine, blond like a Viking and benevolent.

"Now the pair of us are on Pegasus. I am taking the blond Prince to meet my father who is the King. His castle is bathed in light; suddenly we are before the King. I feel happy about introducing the prince to him. The King is happy too and there is no animosity. The palace is light in every place - real home.

"I realise that I cannot stay for I must return to the Mountain. I *am there* and reascend. There is Christ, Himself. I offer myself as the Shining Effervescent Chalice that I now am and which is now me. I hand back the sixth scroll and am given the seventh scroll, which represents my mission in *life.* I turn and descend the stairway and make my way down the mountain to take up this mission."

Anita's Sixth Daydream (Case Ref: G.93):

This lengthy discourse, reporting her experience with the Sixth Daydream, was written up by Anita in two parts as it was necessary to spread the daydream over two consultations. This was the first case where I departed from Desoille's theme deliberately, by mixing the stories of "Beauty and the Beast" and "The Sleeping Beauty", following a pattern set by Marie (see Case C.132 above).This experimental work with the theme of the Sixth Daydream was discussed with Anita beforehand and she was in full concurrence with its use.

"I descended the rest of the mountain and made my way to the stables where I selected the brown horse again. On my journey through the forest there were trees on each side of the track, which I skirted. The horse wanted to break into a trot but I held it back, making it proceed slowly as I did not know whether I wanted to go on. A breeze has blown up and the horse breaks into a trot and I do not check it. I can see the castle in the distance - about two or three miles away but although the horse is now galloping very fast the journey seems to take a long time. It is like a fairy castle with rounded turrets. The roof is not red although tiled, the building itself is greyish and the roof is reddish-brown, ruddy coloured and a turret comes out of the roof. I cross a drawbridge, go through the portcullis, cross the courtyard beyond. Here I tether the horse and go into a hallway where a stairway faces me. I ascend this to find four doors leading off an oblong landing —two of the doors on the left of this, one immediately opposite me and one to my right. I open the door opposite and see a dragon in the room of brownish colour. There are beams on the ceiling and a four-poster bed. The room is cluttered. I (next) open the door on my right; this is a sitting-room with books and is unoccupied. It has pale blue curtains. The first door on my left is a bathroom and unoccupied. The bath is very old - an ancient type. When I open the final door ... the beast is there. The floor of this room is carpeted in green. The fireplace has a mantelpiece. There is a wickerwork chair with a reddish cushion. Leaded light windows with a pelmet, the curtains are rust-coloured. This is a bedroom. There is a round table with flowers and a book on it. It is a pleasant room.

"I decide to enter the Beast's room but when I do it is empty. I go through an adjacent door leading into an oblong room with beamed ceiling and windows down one side with no curtains. The Beast is here. It is small, a grey-coloured creature. It hops about. Its body is round, it has a tail and pointed ears, like a mini-kangaroo. I am not afraid of it and pour liquid over it from my vessel whereupon it disappears. The castle is empty upstairs but I am aware of people downstairs. I see a lady who has apron-like clothing and her hair in a bun at the back — she is elderly — a servant-head. I don't like her. She goes into a kitchen. I enter the library and stay there reading and reading until I actually fall asleep. I wake up to sunlight. Beside me is a flagon of milk so I drink about three-quarters of it. I then look out of the window, after which I go back to the Beast's room. I *see* no beast there yet I *feel* that he is there … yes, he is there. He is not dancing today, he is just quite still. He *is* small."

Do you feel threatened by him in any way?

"I have the chalice! Because the Beast is small I do not feel threatened; yet it has some hold over me. It moves towards me and is jumping up at the chalice. It is smaller than my waist but higher than my knees. Suddenly I feel very, very tired and too late realise that the milk I drank was drugged. The beast with a heave lifts me onto the bed. The daylight is fading. The Beast leaves me there.

"It is now dawn again and there is no sign of the Beast. All day and into the night I remain there alone; it is now my second night alone. I watch dawn break again — the first rays of the dawn. I feel tired but also hungry. The day passes and once again I am left alone.

"I am awakened from sleep by a kiss on my lips. It is *Alan!* (Alan is her husband). Yet there is also that awful woman. I go and seek her out — she *really* resembles my mother — but she hides everywhere. She is dodging me all round the garden. Now Alan is helping me to hunt the woman. There are some raspberry canes in a first pen and we've got her in there and closed the door. The Beast has fled. I could use the vessel to restore the woman if I could make her drink the milk. I stand the vessel on the ground so that the sun shines on it. It is getting the better of the woman and she does not like it. She has her arms up as if screaming and releasing all the anger in her until she is drained. I sit her on a wooden seat in the sun.

"I return to the mountain, return my horse and scale the mountain. This time the Angel comes down. She is taller, upright and slim. The vessel has the sun shining on it, it definitely has no green in it, it is white and glistening in the sun and has gold on it."

Discussing this dream with her she said that the Beast was indecisive and she believed represented to her, her father.

The servant-head who kept hanging about she identified as being her mother. She recalled that when her mother, during a prolonged visit, was in the spare bedroom which was next to hers and Alan's and throughout the period of her mother's occupation of that room Anita felt totally inhibited and unable to make love with her husband.

Rita's Sixth Daydream (Case Ref: M.37):

"I descend the mountain quite effortlessly and make my way to the cottage where I select a palomino and mounting him, set off through the forest. I encounter no problems on my journey and soon reach the castle, which has a drawbridge over a moat. I cross this and make my way towards a large doorway at the far side of the courtyard. I leave my horse here and open the door. A stairway faces me across an entrance hall. I ascend this and find at the top that there are three doors. I select the first door on my right, open it and enter. Beyond is an old dark oak bed that has not been used for a long time. There is a window with a startling light outside. I hear birds singing. The brightness through that window I can only describe as *brilliant white light.* The room does not smell musty. It is empty.

"I open the second door. Inside is a pretty little bed with a patchwork quilt. There is a little girl in it. She is startled and wonders why she has been disturbed. She is very fair; about six years old. There is no sign of the Beast.

"I open the third door and there is the Beast ... a two-legged beast. He is like Dr. Jeckyl but he is dressed as a mediaeval knight, covered in armour. He is armed and his face is covered by his helmet that has a visor. He is holding a lance. He doesn't look too ferocious and invites me into the room. He is telling me, "I wish you no harm" and offers me a drink. I remove his helmet — he is a very young man with reddish hair. He is rather innocent, happy. We are having a drink together now.

"I am feeling very sleepy. Too late I realise that I have been drugged. The young man carries me to the first bedroom and puts me on the bed. Although the bed is low I can see the blue sky through the window and gradually the sky darkens and night descends. A swan appears outside the window and seems to be very friendly and I feel comforted.

"Suddenly in my sleep I am aware of someone kissing my mouth and I awake, released from the effects of the drug. The person who has released me is like the young man grown up. He is older. He has a girl with him who is wearing green and white. She has brown hair and she looks as if she could be somewhere between eighteen and twenty-five years old."

What's happening?

"I am staying with this couple for a while before journeying back. The courtyard is now like a rose garden, like a formal French garden full of red roses. The other side (of the castle) is palatial, higher ceilings with more light and air. Quite a lot of marble inside. Very opulent with works of art, paintings, sculptures and things. There is an area where horses are kept and I discover my palomino! I leave the castle and make my way back, return the horse at the cottage and ascend the mountain on foot to the very peak. I am wearing a blue dress!

"I am climbing the golden stairway and here I meet a white figure — almost formless; white *energy* — doesn't need form. I hand the Sixth scroll to it and in my hands is placed the Seventh Scroll, which I am told is my *Life Scroll.* the Chalice is almost weightless; its like the colour of lightning — as if it has its own life. I am now being given a cover — like a white mist but with more life than mist — like being washed with dry water ... ethereal washing. I feel that I have passed some form of initiation ..."

Sylvia's Sixth Daydream (Case Ref: M.164):

" ... I have selected a chestnut horse and I am journeying through the forest. I soon see the castle in a clearing through the trees. The castle is not built on a hill but on flat ground but around it there is a moat. The drawbridge is old, almost dilapidated. The castle has four turrets, one at each corner. As I approach, the drawbridge is lowered and I cross into a courtyard beyond. Through a big door I now go and ascend a large stairway leading off the hall. At the top there are six doors. I open the first of these and see that the room beyond is very large and well-furnished with big drapes at all the windows, a lovely desk, antique ornaments and in one corner a big bed with a red fabric canopy. There is also a table in the room laden with fruit. I like this room. There is no-one in it so I leave the room and enter the second doorway. This is cold and bare; it has curtained windows and a little lamp beside a makeshift bed. The room is empty and I sense that this is the Guard's room.

"The third door when opened reveals a family drawing-room with an old, very old piano. The furnishings are rich and there are noises in the room of children - in Edwardian dress with ringlets in their hair. There is a mother and father with three young children and two older ones but I cannot make out their features. It is like a scene from a Christmas card.

"I tip-toe out of the room and open the fourth door. Beyond is an empty room with no furnishings whatsoever. I open door five which opens onto a blank, dark room like a sort of kitchen with a large Welsh Dresser, a scrubbed kitchen table and deep shelves. There is no-one in the room. I open the last door and I shut it again."

Why?

"Because I heard a terrible roar from the beast. The beast is definitely in that room!"

Did you not see him?

"I could not see him when I opened the door; he must have been like a ghost. I am afraid to enter".

You have the chalice. Remember in a dream anything can happen. Open the door!

"I am afraid. It is as if he is a vacuum and will suck me in if I open the door but I have to enter. I have to see this through. I am opening the door and entering the room but immediately I feel myself and the chalice forced flat against the wall. I am immobile. The Beast is hurling itself about, like a line, (a live electric cable). The Chalice has fallen to the floor.

What's happening?

"The Beast has slowed down and has become visible to the eye. His purpose is to take me for his bride. In appearance he looks like Jamie (her boy friend). He picks me up and carries me to the corner of the room where there is an old four-poster bed. He forces me to take a drink from a goblet, then lays me on the bed and leaves the room.

"The ceiling above me is cracked. I can see through the window beside the bed and the sky is blue. The beast does not return and the day passes into night. I now can see nothing as it is very dark and everywhere is silent. It is a long night but at last daylight comes again. I must have slept a little. I feel confused. I accepted the drink because I thought it was Jamie. I feel as if I ought to get up and walk out of the room but the drink must have been drugged because I cannot move.

"All day long I lay there and now it is getting dark again. I would rather the Beast come back than just being here waiting. I am afraid but would rather have *something* than *nothing*; get it over with. Again I sleep fitfully through the silence and the blackness of the night. Still no one comes.

"Now it is dawn again. Somewhere I can hear a woman screaming; she is screaming and screaming in pain. The beast is armed, perhaps. I feel someone kiss my lips. It is not the beast; it could be anybody, could be Jamie. The face above me is smiling. The smile is like Jamie's. I can move. I can see the chalice. It looks smaller. If I pick it up I'll want it so I decide to leave it there".

What's happening?

"I have changed my mind and pick it up and leave the room and the castle and make my way through the forest and back to the mountain which I climb with ease. The figure on the stairway is the same as before but I see his features clearly now. He is bearded, his beard and his hair being a reddish-brown. He has green eyes and a very peaceful air about him. He is friendly towards me and tells me that I have completed all the assignments, this being the last. The chalice is gold with an inscription on it and a lovely watermark comprised of green wavy lines. I want to get on the horse and travel anywhere, travel in the opposite direction to everything I have known. I feel excited and mount the horse and we set off at a gallop, faster and faster. The wind is blowing in my hair and I feel exhilarated, *free."*

Michaela's Sixth Daydream (Case Ref: O.45):

"At the cottage I select the white mare. How cool it is under the shade of the trees. Birds fly above me and all about are woodland creatures — there some squirrels, there some rabbits and some reindeer. In a clearing in the depths of the forest is a castle. It has a deep moat all around it. Its windows are rounded with a sort of cross in the centre of their stonework. There is a large tower on the left. The drawbridge is down. I cross it and enter the main hall where ahead I see five doors. One door is larger than the rest. I push the door open and enter. There is a huge basket in the corner, takes up half the room. I see a huge rounded black thing, blue glaring eyes, long thick tail, lots of sharp claws. It fills half the room. I feel like tackling it. With the chalice held in front of me I move towards it. It stares at me. I touch it with my chalice. It shrinks, then disappears. I decide to check out the other rooms. One contains a bunk bed and wardrobe; the next contains a double bed with a curtain around it on a rail, and a wardrobe; a small bathroom and toilet leads off this room. The next room is a sort of lounge-diner and has a TV in front of a fireplace, a settee and comfortable armchairs and there is a dining table and chairs too. The final room is a kitchen with old fashioned cooking equipment. I go back to the lounge-diner and on the table there is a flagon of wine. I drink some of it and sit down on the settee as I feel so tired. I fall asleep. I am asleep like the fabled sleeping princess but someone has come into the room and kissed me to awaken me. It is *Martin*!" (Martin is her boy friend).

Beryl's Sixth Daydream (Case Ref: W.154):

"This time I select the black horse which looks fast and powerful and head out across the desert to find the castle. After some riding without event, I come across the castle that I am seeking. It looks more like the Taj Mehal than a castle. Its gates are made of black metal but I open these and cross the inner courtyard where there are two doors; the main door and a smaller side door. Leaving the black stallion, I enter the main doorway and find myself in a hall from which leads a staircase. I climb the stairs, which lead up to a balcony that has five doors. Instinctively I *know* which room is occupied by the beast and head straight for the door and open it. Inside the room is a lion making a lot of noise; he holds a very large fork, like a trident, in his hand (he has *hands* not *paws*). I am suddenly aware that a black panther is slinking up behind me and although the lion seems friendly, the panther might be evil.

"I turn my back on the lion as I feel that I can trust it and I face the challenge of the panther. This creature has massive yellow eyes but I feel that it constitutes no threat. In fact, it lays down on the floor and I am able to tickle it under its chin. The chalice is behind me, beside the lion. When I turn to retrieve it, however, the lion I saw is no longer there but its place has been taken by the beast. The real beast is different - it has the body of a man but the head of a lion. The beast has long nails but nondescript eyes. It is looking at me in a way that makes me nervous and as I try to keep my gaze on the beast I begin to freeze all over, so that now I am unable to move my legs or my arms ... or my head. I can move my eyes and I can see and hear that is all. I am laying opposite a window and able to see the setting sun. The room is now dark but I can make out the panther's eyes, glowing. The panther is moving towards me. It is licking me.

"I am aware of other movement and can hear the sound of someone else entering the room. I think that it is the lion-man-beast who is bending over me and kissing me but he has turned into a handsome man — dark haired, olive skinned and very handsome. I am now able to move so I reach out and retrieve my chalice.

"I leave the castle accompanied by both the lion and the panther and return to the mountain which I ascend without difficulty. I then climb the golden stairway where Christ awaits me. I hand Him the Sixth Scroll and He in turn gives me another scroll, the seventh, which I am told is my ongoing assignment, my life. I salute Christ with the Chalice, which is now of pure gold, very elaborate with carvings on the outside. It is shining very brightly. I descend the stairway and the mountain without difficulty."

Colin's Sixth Daydream (Case Ref: L.70):

" ... I select the brown horse again. The woman who occupies the cottage resembles both my mother and my father in looks although this person is very definitely female. I do not want her to accompany me to the castle of the sleeping princess as I fear that she may be harmed by the beast there so I set out alone.

"I make my way through the forest and soon reach the castle of the sleeping princess. The castle has high battlements and turrets and is surrounded by a deep, dark moat. The drawbridge is down and I start to cross it only to discover that the portcullis is barring my way. I see a horse drawn cart approaching and decide that I will hide myself in the cart when the driver stops the horse in front of the portcullis. He is a very ordinary man and his attention is on the portcullis, which is being raised to let him through. I climb unnoticed into the cart and discover that it is full of food and is obviously to be delivered to the castle. As soon as the portcullis is raised and the horse and cart allowed through I leap from the cart and enter the castle. I run up the stairs and immediately I am confronted by the beast, resembling a large black bear. He tries to bar my way to the room, outside which he stands, and although I could quite easily run him through with my sword, instead I use the sword to cut the floor away beneath his feet and he tumbles down the hole I have made. I enter the room where I see the sleeping princess on a settee. She is very good-looking, red-haired, bluish coloured eyes and she is wearing a white wedding-gown. I kiss her and she awakes from her sleep. She tells me that the beast has been holding others of her family and servants prisoner and that by awakening her I have also released them all."

What is the matter?

"I am worrying about the beast".

Do you think it might attack you or the princess?

"No. I am worried that I might have injured it".

What are you going to do?

"I am going to find it. When I cut away the floor it fell to the floor below. I make my way down the stairs and find the beast below. It is injured and bleeding from the knees. With the help of some of the servants I manage to get the beast onto the cart and then I mount my horse and start back for the cottage and where I know that the beast can be cared for. The man driving the cart follows me. Soon we reach the cottage and after satisfying myself that the beast is properly taken care of I return the brown horse to its stable and make my way back to the mountain. I climb it easily and then climb the stairway where I am met by Pure Light. When I raise my sword in salutation I notice that it now has a silver blade with a gold hilt in which is set a red jewel. The hilt is patterned in the shape of heads of people.

"I am told that this was my sixth assignment and I must now make my way back down the stairway and the mountain to undertake the seventh assignment which is the adventure of my life before me ..."

Carl's Sixth Daydream (Case Ref: M.130):

Before the Daydream he recalled an experience with his mother: her leaving him for the first time when he had been taken to play-school. It seems that he went into a state of near hysteria when she left him and he had to be sent back home because he screamed so much.

In the daydream he found his mother on the outskirts of the forest and was then led by her to the castle of the sleeping beauty. His description of the castle was typical, stone walls, moat and drawbridge. The drawbridge was down and he entered the courtyard beyond and then entered the main doorway that led to "a big hall lined with shields and swords". He climbed a stairway that "curves to the left" but at the top found his "way barred by a knight". He hits the knight across the legs with his curved sword hoping to bring him down as he "does not really want to harm him". However, the knight starts to rise to his feet again and is obviously going to make it a fight to the death so Carl, using the straight sword, decapitates him. He explains that there are three rooms and the Sleeping Beauty is located in the third of these. He describes her as being "young, fair-haired and beautiful—like the young girl who was on the shaft of light above the mountain".

He kisses her on the lips and awakens her from her sleep, which releases her and all the other people in the castle from the spell they had been under. He then kneels before her and hands her the straight sword in silent homage. She introduces him to her father, the King and he, in turn, introduces her to his mother and then has to take his temporary leave of them to return to the mountain. He describes his ascent of both the mountain and the shaft of light, this time, as being without problems. He meets both the wise old man and the young girl who smiles at him in recognition. He knows that he has successfully accomplished the sixth assignment and raises his sword in salutation. He discovers that his sword is neither like the curved nor the straight one but "now being of pure gold, more ceremonial in appearance."

Warren's Sixth Daydream (Case Ref: S.164):

"Again I select the horse with the white nose and set off to find the castle of the Sleeping Beauty. The journey through the pine forest is uneventful and I soon reach the castle. It is just like the castle illustrated in children's fairy tales. The drawbridge is down so I enter the courtyard and ahead of me are two entrances to the castle itself. Leaving the horse, I enter the doorway on the left and find myself in a sort of arena. Two men are locked in combat. One resembles Neanderthal man, while the other is dressed as a knight and is wearing armour. The Knight now has the caveman on the floor; he is holding a trident in his right hand and a net in his left hand. The Knight pushes the trident into the throat of the caveman, who has a big, fat, red tongue and keeps lifting up his head and gasping. Two monks are standing by watching this combat. I notice a gap in the wall of the arena leading to a narrow passage. I am entering it now but it is so narrow that I am having to move along it sideways. It leads back to the castle grounds on the other side of the moat and I have to start again across the drawbridge into the courtyard. The Knight is now *there* and at first he seems smaller but grows again to normal size. The scene is identical - the conflict between the Knight and the Neanderthal man, except that the Knight is now armed with a short Roman sword. Although he slashes at the face and neck of the Neanderthal man that one just laughs and will not die! I offer my sword to the Knight who accepts it and proceeds to chop off the head of the Neanderthal. The Knight is handing me back my sword, which is now glowing. The Knight proceeds to lead me into the castle and to a stone room with a 4-poster bed on which I can see the sleeping princess through the curtains. The Knight is now holding a mace in his hand. The princess is very lovely and I bend over her and kiss her on her lips, noticing as I do so that the curtains have gone. The princess awakes, shakes her head and then smiles as she puts her arms around me and seems very happy. The Knight sheds his armour and stands in fine robes, well groomed, a handsome fresh complexioned man — the rightful owner of the castle.

"The journey back is over hills with a void, a chasm which I am able to fly over with a magic cloak I am wearing. But I have to leave the horse with the white nose behind. I fly over the pine forest too and soon reach the mountain in this way. I climb it easily and then the stairway beyond to the seventh stair. My sword is glowing all around the blade and hilt. I am aware that my sixth mission has ended but I must now return to the foot of the mountain to carry on with my life below.

" I begin to descend the stairs. Now someone is getting in my way".

(Long silence)

Who is it?

"It is the witch — no, my mother —but she looks like Jenny."

Another silence.

What's happening?

"I am shrinking and as I shrink, so Jenny grows bigger. I don't know what to do".

In a dream anything is possible. ***Do something!***

"I have descended to the second stair and by doing this I am back to my full height. She is still barring my way."

Can you use your sword?

"The sword I am holding is an old wooden one but I touch her with it. This is causing her to have a fit, screaming and shouting. I push the wooden sword into her stomach, not to pierce her but to push her. She is laying down now and I have put my foot on her. I no longer have the wooden sword but my *real* sword, which I am holding in my left hand. I have descended the stairs and am now beginning my descent of the mountain but the path is practically vertical and I am having to place my sword between two protruding rocks and am lowering myself by rope to the base. I have reached the base but here it is like the sea and I move away from it and into the desert that is now quite peaceful with a sort of glow about it, a white-golden sort of glow. Suddenly my white horse appears and greets me. I am so pleased to see him and am putting my arms round his neck. Now my father and mother are there followed by my sister, brother-in-law and my three nephews. Jenny is sitting astride the horse. A cave appears and when I look into it I see first an igloo and then an Eskimo and finally a native hut. These disappear and are replaced by a stream which cascades like a waterfall down towards the forest. It is beautiful. I recognise this as a part of Canada I once visited."

Stuart's Sixth Daydream (Case Ref: T.68):

He sees his mother at the base of the mountain but decides to make his way alone. He finds the castle of the Sleeping Beauty without difficulty and describes it as being a typical castle of the period with a moat and drawbridge. The drawbridge is down and the portcullis is open but he has some difficulty in entering as something seemed to be holding him back. He uses his sword to free himself from the force that was holding him back. He manages to drag himself through the opening and enters the castle where he sees before him a flight of stone steps, which he begins to climb. This does not prove too difficult except for the final step that seems larger than the others and requires more effort. Ahead are fifteen doors; the first six of these "are all red and are all the same" (look identical). The seventh door is *almost* invisible. He believes that this is the room where the sleeping beauty is so enters the room but his way is barred by a dragon, "similar in appearance to the one in the cave". The dragon pushes him out of the room but Simon recovers himself and returns to the room, ready to fight the dragon. However, the dragon appears to be resting — "he is snoring but not asleep". Stuart does not trust the dragon and although it appears to be slow he knows that it can be very agile. He uses the sword, cutting and thrusting and after a fierce battle manages to subdue the beast. The Sleeping beauty "is dressed in blue, a blue which matches her lovely eyes. She has long golden hair". He kisses her and she wakes from her sleep, deeply grateful to him. She introduces him to her father, the King, who is very pleased at what has happened.

Stuart takes the princess to meet his mother and decides to return to the mountain through the desert which he describes as now being fertile, transformed. Leaving the princess in the temporary care of his mother, he ascends the mountain and the stairway beyond where he hands over the sixth scroll to Jesus. He describes his sword as being a radiant blue and shining ..."

In the next and concluding Chapter the *purpose* of the six daydreams will be explained and their affect on each of these clients.

* * *

CHAPTER 11

In this, the concluding part of my book, I would like to explain what Desoille describes as the purpose of each of the six daydreams. Before doing this, however, I must emphasise once again the fact that the therapist may spend more than six sessions with each client working through the six daydreams. This proves necessary because many clients are unable to achieve the desired result on their first attempt. As Desoille explains: "It may therefore be necessary to go back over the same theme as many as four or five times before the images that provoke anxiety are completely drained of their painful affective charge". He goes on to say: "When they have been overcome, we can consider the situation as being thoroughly analysed. At that point it is generally reasonable for us to consider that we have had the subject face every possible kind of life situation and that the exploration of his habitual responses to these situations has been completed."

Further, the sequence of the six directed daydreams constitutes but the *first phase* of treatment. The next, the second phase, involves showing the client "new and *underdeveloped* response possibilities. First, he must be made aware of them; then, he must be helped to cultivate and to convert them into new habits. These problems are also worked out on a completely imaginary level."

The final or third phase is where the client is trained to move from the realm of imagination into that of *reality*[1] . This aspect may require several sessions in therapy; just how many will depend largely on the abilities of both the client and the therapist and the rapport which has been established between them. Briefly, it is time spent in discussion, reconstruction, sometimes in destruction but always with the goal of positive *construction*.

The theme of the First Daydream in which the ascent of the mountain and beyond is undertaken also involves the client being presented with a sword, in the case of a man, or a chalice or vessel in the case of a woman. The purpose of this daydream is to enable the client to confront his *characteristics*. For example, when a man is asked to describe the sword, in symbolic language this is equivalent to asking him what he thinks of himself as a man, in the broadest sense of the term. As Desoille explains: "The images that I offer my subjects actually correspond to rather precise questions. They are couched in what Politzer has called the *intimate language*; the universal language of dream symbolism. Although the subject *knows* this language and replies

[1] *Reality or real* - Charles Rycroft in his *Critical Dictionary of Psychoanalysis* says that "Psychoanalysis combines allegiance to the common-sense or natural scientific view that a distinction can be made between *external* phenomena which are 'real' or 'really there' and *mental* phenomena which are subjective images, with the conviction that mental phenomena are of dynamic consequence and therefore, in some sense also real. As a result it uses 'real' to mean either *objectively present* or *subjectively significant.* It also assumes that all objective phenomena occupy a space external to the subject which is called *external reality* (or, less frequently *objective reality*) and that images, thoughts, phantasies, feelings, etc., occupy a space inside the subject which is called *internal reality* or *psychic reality* - internal and external reality both being realms in which things are and processes occur ..."

in it, albeit unconsciously, he is not aware of its semantics[2]. In order to understand the client and to help him to understand himself, *therapist and client together* must translate the symbols of this secret language into words of everyday language." It is for this reason that the person is asked to write a full account of each of his directed daydreams and to bring it along to the next session so that its content can be analysed as completely as possible.

The interpretation requires "both sensitivity and finesse" and can only be accomplished with the active collaboration of the subject. Desoille emphasises that it should be based upon three things:

1. a thorough anamnesis[3] of the subject's past;
2. ideas which the subject spontaneously associates to the content of his directed daydream, and
3. any other ideas which arise during the session, and I would add: *including those prompted by nocturnal dreams.*

He warns, of course, that the interpretation is to be considered valid only if the patient feels it to be correct and fully agrees with it. Interpretation, as Desoille admits, will be based upon everything that Freud, Jung and Adler have taught about how our feelings find expression. Based upon my experience with the Desoille Daydreams I can state quite categorically that Desoille's work has added its unique contribution to the process of understanding. In Chapter 5, we saw that "one of the important advantages of the directed daydream technique is that it provokes intense emotional reactions very easily". This being indispensable for the attainment of certain states of consciousness and so far as effective therapy is concerned, "... is essential to the achievement of a cure".

Although it is pertinent during the course of the client's first directed daydream to remind him that "in a dream anything is possible" thus avoiding anything which may create anxiety, this is not so in the second directed daydream. Before the client embarks on the second directed daydream he is warned beforehand that he is going to be asked to imagine a descent that will quite likely stimulate the appearance of unpleasant, possibly horrible, images but it is impressed upon him that he should face up to them bravely since that is the only way to discover the origin and character of one's anxieties. Only by doing so can he then learn how to conquer them and to dispel them gradually. The purpose of the second daydream is that of confronting one's more suppressed characteristics and this is accomplished by, as Desoille puts it, "a rather random probing of the . . . unconscious. It corresponds to the questions: *what is going on in the depths of your personality? what painful feelings are capable of upsetting you?*" In general, feelings of fear arise quite quickly. Frequently the 'monster of the depths' will resemble an octopus, sometimes a sea serpent, a conga

[2] *Semantics* - Originally, that branch of philology that is concerned with the meaning of words. Nowadays, often, the study of *meaning* in general. According to Szasz (1961), Home (1966) and Rycroft (1966), psychoanalysis, or at least some parts of it, is a semantic theory since it shows that *dreams* and *neurotic symptoms* have meaning.

[3] *Anamnesis* - Medical term for the history of an illness as given by the patient at consultation, i.e. for his recall of the relevant past.

Eel or other threatening creature. The client is encouraged to face and subdue the beast or tame it. Subsequently, when the client is retracing his way to the ledge, the monster follows him and the client then has to "tap" the monster once again thus inducing a metamorphosis in it. It is the occurrence of this metamorphosis, which *reveals its true identity.*

In the first two daydreams the client has to confront aspects of himself or herself. By contrast, Daydreams 3 and 4, involving the search for a sorcerer or magician, or a witch in a cave "take more specific directions from the more specific nature of the themes". Their purpose is that of coming to terms with the parent of the opposite sex and the parent of one's own sex. All the images occur spontaneously but instead of waiting for them to arise "they can be evoked by the therapist and used to direct the course of the daydream to explore the client's habitual responses to others". By so doing neurotic patterns and their origins are exposed. Similarly, "maladaptive" reactions can be changed, first in the imagination and then in reality. These series of images are called "archetypal *chains*". Jungian analysts are familiar with them "but only as they have arisen spontaneously from folklore traditions ... they have no methods for evoking them intentionally so that they can be studied *in vivo* and used Therapeutically".

Desoille's own description of the Directed Daydream is that it is an intermediate hypnoidal state which shades between wakefulness and sleep and is essentially a device for tapping the inexhaustible reservoir in which we accumulate, during the course of our lives, anxieties, fears, desires and hopes. He adds that these factors maintain their determining influence over our ongoing behaviour whenever we have to cope with the external world. In this book I have given illustrations of my own experience with clients, using not only the Directed Daydreams but also other techniques ranging from *implosive therapy* to Freudian *Free Association* and *Hypnosis.* It has been evident to me that this "inexhaustible reservoir" to which Desoille refers also includes experiences during our lives which I believe fall under the general heading of *unconscious experiences.* From the illustrations I have given it will have been evident that most of us have experiences of so-called unconsciousness during our lives. The duration of time of such experiences may range from a brief moment of unconsciousness where an intense pain causes us to withdraw consciousness for a second or two, to more severe conditions and injuries embracing days or even months of unconsciousness. Surgical operations, including teeth extractions, under general anaesthetic are included in these unconscious experiences. However, none of us during these experiences is *totally* unconscious, for if we were it would be impossible for us, under hypnosis or any other technique for that matter, to recall them. That we *can* recall *in detail* our surroundings and the events taking place when we are "unconscious" has been demonstrated to me over and over again by my clients during session. Indeed, it is only when such moments are restored to our consciousness, our understanding, through *abreaction*[4] that our minds are "completely

[4] *abreaction* - The discharge of emotion attaching to a previously repressed experience, (repression being the defence mechanism process by which an unacceptable impulse or idea is rendered *unconscious*).

drained of their painful affective charge" and the release has brought back into use the trapped energy or "charge".

Desoille believes that through the Directed Daydream technique we are able to explore "an entirely new world that was unknown to both Freud and Adler" and but glimpsed by Jung, the visionary who has "described it in a very sketchy fashion by drawing upon traditional legends".

Dream imagery is sub-divided into "levels" by Desoille, as follows:

1. Images of reality and images of nocturnal dreams.
2. Images from fables and myths. Those most commonly found in directed daydreams involving *descent* are witches, sorcerers, magicians, demons, dragons and the like, while those involving *ascent* are wise men, fairies, angels, winged horses, with Christ, the Virgin and God the Father appearing in the dreams of people who inhabit a cultural milieu infused with Christian imagery.
3. Finally, there are *mystical* images because they do not represent any familiar objects but are composed of more or less vibrant impressions of light 'though they sometimes give the impression of being alive. They lack all objective representational character and can be understood only in terms of the *feelings* the person has while "seeing" them, such feelings ranging from calmness and serenity to enthusiasm and jubilation and even to adoration. In fact, the only comparable experiences are the visions and accompanying feelings that have been described by mystics.

Dr. Israel Regardie tells us that it is important for the would-be magus to undertake psychological counselling before, or as an adjunct to, esoteric training. While Mark Stavish, MA, in *Problems on the Path of Return: Pathology in Kabbalistic and Alchemical Practices* claims that "the majority of all so-called magical, alchemical, or esoteric work, as much as 90% of it, is nothing more than glorified psychotherapy". He also adds: "While many therapists and esotericists are familiar with the writings of Carl Jung and have applied them in some form to their respective work, the realm of therapy that is most important to esoteric students during practical alchemy and ritual work is more closely akin to Freud than Jung". He points out that the combined systems of Jung and Freud will only give a glimpse into the interior worlds, as they lack effective techniques for the kind of initiation that most esotericists seek. In my opinion, Robert Desoille's Directed Daydreams move the process forward to provide an effective technique since each Daydream is in itself *an initiation.*

Part of my work in the Social Services involved report-writing and it was not uncommon to discover, at the end of a day spent in visiting people in their homes, that I had some twenty or so reports to write up. This I found was made much easier by the employment of simple "memory pegs". By memory pegs I mean a brief note of something scribbled on a pad at the time of the visit, which when I read some hours later, possibly even a day later, would enable me to recall clearly to mind all the important facts needed for the report. For example, if I wrote the words "ginger cat" I would see not only the ginger cat in my mind's eye but also its owner, the person whom I had visited, other persons in the family who had been present at the time, the condition or state of their environment, and what had taken place during the interview. Sometimes, of course, the appearance of the person whom I had interviewed became the memory-peg if there were any unusual features such as a limb missing, a patch over one eye, a large nose, etc. The system became very effective, and it certainly worked for me. It is not difficult to understand why it did because it followed another natural law of the mind, *linking*.

The computer contains memory banks just as we, its creators, have memory banks. Both the computer's and our own memory banks depend upon *input*. The input of our memory bank is all our continuing experiences every moment of our lives. The miracle of it all is that this astronomical amount of data is capable of being stored in our memory banks with or without conscious effort on our part. We can learn verses in a poem, the lyrics of a song, or our lines in a play, we can learn methods on how to solve mathematical problems, how to construct and operate mechanical devices of varying complexity but whatever we are doing which appears to be occupying our attention, are we not are also recording an enormous amount of other environmental information through our physical senses, as well as our mental processes? This additional input will embrace colours, shapes, temperature, sounds, smells, tastes, touch, etc., yet somehow *all o*f this data is filed or stored in our memory banks for our possible future use. Such a filing system is far more complex, far more detailed, than anything we have in our desktop computers! Our ability to subsequently recall this data will depend very much upon *linking*. This is an ingenious system with which we are gifted.

However, the system is not without its problems. So far, we have looked at the *conscious* and positive use of linking but linking can and does take place without our conscious knowledge when it is triggered by *similarities*. For example, Appendix III of my first report, in September 1983, to the British Medical Association, *Analysis of Psychotherapy, Hypnotherapy and Orthomolecular Treatments carried out between 1974 and 1982 in England, Canada and the United States of America,* contained an illustration (case Ref: D.2) of the effective use of Freud's Free Association technique which I have reproduced in Appendix **(1)** at the end of this book. Another Example of it was given in "habit conditioning" in Chapter 3.

By now it should be clear that *linking* is a natural law or function of mind and whilst its negative aspect may produce a long chain of related incidents or experiences connected to a physically or emotionally painful or unpleasant *repression*, on the other hand in the very existence of that chain we are provided with the key, the positive aspect, of being able to tap in at any point on the chain, knowing that ultimately it will lead to our being able gradually (or rapidly at times!) to uncover the fundamental or basic repressed experience that holds the charge, the energy, needing to be released through abreaction.

By the *linking* of all of the missions of the six Directed Daydreams through *the Scroll* as I have mentioned in Chapter 7, I have made use of this law of the mind. It is a refinement that I introduced from my experience of working with Freud's *Free*

Association technique in Practice. Nevertheless, my "adherence to a different theoretical explanation" as Desoille puts it, did indeed lead to the discovery of "new procedures and (thus) shorten the time of treatment".

The theme of Daydream 5, the descent into the cave of the fabled dragon, is that of coming to terms with the constraints imposed upon one by society. It is identifying *symbolically* with those areas of societal conditioning and their *constraining* influence upon us. Desoille believes that the dragon "stands for all the prohibitions imposed (upon us) by (our) cultural milieu". He goes on to explain: "First ... there are the restrictions imposed by the family, then there are those which arise from (our) social class and from ... vocational commitments .. . and finally, the Nation, too, (which) imposes its limitations on the individual". It is only by facing this dragon that we are able to come to terms with these constraints and gradually, by accepting them for what they are, regaining our freedom mentally and spiritually. Desoille adds that if a *treasure* appears in the directed daydream, it represents the various mental and spiritual potentialities, which the person has been prevented from developing because of those numerous prohibitions. If there are any prisoners held by the dragon, these too are symbolic for they stand for that part of our own sensitivity which makes it possible for us to empathise with our counterpart (*Anima* or *Animus* in Jungian terms, describing the unconscious *female* image in men and the unconscious *male* image in women) and subsequently live in harmony with it for "if this ability is not developed, contact with the opposite sex tends to be strained".

Daydream 6 is the story of the Sleeping Beauty and will be conducted differently for men and women. The male client is asked to evoke the memory of an experience he actually had with his mother, whether agreeable or unpleasant. He is then asked to have his mother accompany him through the forest to search for the castle of the Sleeping Beauty. When the castle is found, the man is required to leave his mother in the reception hall while he goes upstairs alone to find the bedroom of the Sleeping Beauty and awaken her. Usually the male client will quite spontaneously take on the role of the prince of the fable and in emulating the prince, achieves adult maturity. He is asked to offer his sword to the princess, Sleeping Beauty "as a token of his esteem", then, making an ascension in her company, to tour the castle, finally making a descent to the reception hall to meet his mother, "whereupon Sleeping Beauty welcomes her future mother-in-law to her home and leads her to a wing (of the castle) which has been reserved especially for her". Symbolically, the man has been permitted to take a wife by his mother.

In the case of a woman, she has to imagine that she herself is the Sleeping Beauty, asleep on a bed and aware that someone is approaching her bedside and to tell what happens. Usually there is the awakening with a kiss but not infrequently, although completely imaginary, "this theme can give rise to extremely dramatic scenes" as Desoille puts it. After her awakening the Sleeping Beauty ascends with her suitor, the prince, to meet her father, the king.

The theme is employed "in order to direct the (client's) efforts toward the resolution of the oedipal conflict, that is, Freud's classic discovery that a person may have come of age but still be emotionally attached to the parent of the opposite sex".

Rycroft says of the *Oedipus Complex* that it is a "group of largely *unconscious* ideas and feelings centring around the wish to possess the parent of the opposite sex and eliminate that of the same sex. The complex emerges during the *oedipal phase* of development (the pre-oedipal phases, according to classical theory, being narcissistic. The oedipal phase on the other hand being seen as that where the capacity for *object-love* emerges). Freud first mentioned the Oedipus complex in a letter to Fliess in 1897, following a self-analysis conducted after the death of his father but it was first published in the *Interpretation of Dreams* in 1900.

The sixth daydream, however, can accomplish far more than that of reaching the state of sexual maturity in the physical and emotional senses. It can also be a means of bringing about the *Alchemical Wedding*, the balancing not only of the male and female *within* us but also the harmonious reconciliation of our spiritual and material aspects in the matter of our spiritual *psychosynthesis*. Roberto Assagioli explains in *Self-Realisation and Psychological Disturbances* that sometimes difficulties are caused or aggravated by an excessive personal effort to hasten the higher realisation "by the forceful inhibition and repression of the sexual and aggressive drives", an attempt which "only serves to produce an intensification of the (inner) conflict with resultant tension and neurotic symptoms". He states that such an attitude is often the outcome of "moral and religious conceptions too rigid and dualistic which engender condemnation of the natural drives, viewed as 'bad' or 'sinful' ... ". He points out that although some people may have *consciously* abandoned that attitude, they are still *unconsciously* conditioned producing a dichotomy, which in turn causes oscillation between the extremes of *suppression* and the uncontrolled *expression* of all drives. The solution lies along the lines of harmonious integration of all drives, first through the proper subordination and co-ordination and then through the transformation and sublimation of the *excessive or unused quota of energy.*

He warns us: "The achievement of this integration is not only impeded but can be greatly facilitated by the activation of the superconscious functions, by the realisation of the Self, because those larger and higher interests act as a magnet which draws up the libido or psychic energy invested in the "lower" drives. Moreover, when one of the specific functions of the Self, the will, is recognised and utilised it too can contribute effectively, by means of its regulating and controlling power, to the harmonious integration, to the bio-synthesis of the *whole* human being" , a process which can be greatly helped and hastened by certain "psychological and psychophysical techniques ... applied by therapists and educators but which can also be self-applied" of which he later mentions Desoille's *"Rêve éveillé"*.

Desoille makes it clearly understood that "a period of training of the subject in the technique of the directed daydream is necessary" the duration of which may vary from one person to the next but "just as in the establishment of a classical conditional reflex, isolation and repetition play their roles". He goes on to say that the training procedure in itself has a curative effect, even in the early sessions since both the will and the attention are re-educated, forcing the subject to make a concerted effort in attending to his mental imagery. He adds that after the person "has found these images and experienced these adult feelings, he has undergone a genuine emotional maturation". Naturally, when the person understands and has accepted the technique he is able to "practise it in fantasy on his own". He frankly admits later that "the patient cures himself; the most that the psychotherapist (or educator) can do is to teach him how to do it".

* * *

It now remains for me to explain how Desoille's six daydreams helped those twelve clients whose progress we have been following. After each psychotherapy session the client is asked to write a full account of the directed daydream he or she has just completed and bring it along to the next appointment so that it can be discussed and its content analysed as completely as possible.

The interpretation requires both sensitivity and finesse and can only be done with the active collaboration of the client. As I have emphasised earlier, the interpretation will be considered *valid* only if the client feels it to be correct and fully agrees with it. At the risk of being criticised for repeating myself, which I am about to do because of its importance, I wish to re-emphasise Desoille's explanation that the interpretation will be based upon the three following essential points:

1. a thorough anamnesis of the client's past,
2. ideas which he associates quite spontaneously to the content of his directed daydream and
3. any other ideas that may arise during the session.

The client's symbolism is unique to him or her and therefore the following accounts contain no interpretations that can be applied to dreams in general. To one client a serpent in his dream may be a symbol of something quite beautiful while to another client it may be symbolic of something sinister, or to be feared.

Carl Jung in *Man and his Symbols* states "No dream symbol can be separated from the individual who dreams it and there is no definite or straightforward interpretation of any dream".

I therefore make no attempt in the following accounts to give what might be termed as universal dream interpretations. The meanings, apart from a few general symbols, which may be recognised, are those that were peculiar and significant to each client.

Anna (Case Ref. G.118):

After Daydreams 3 and 4, Anna experienced a recurring nocturnal dream about the furniture in her room being huge. She said it was like Alice in Wonderland when Alice became smaller and smaller and her surroundings loomed larger and larger in consequence. Her own interpretation of the dream was that she felt that because things tended to loom unnecessarily large to her, in her real life situation she reacted to situations with unnecessary fear.

Anna felt that she had missed out during her early childhood, having been brought up by elderly grandparents who expected her to do household chores at quite an early age. She resented them in consequence and blamed them for having missed that normal part of her childhood, which other children of her age had seemed to enjoy. Hence, her images of the wizard and the witch as being those of elderly people. The prisoners include a young girl of about three (herself), two small boys (other, male, aspects of herself), an unhealthy, pallid woman (her own deceased mother) and a very old man (her grandfather who in real life was somewhat dominated by her grandmother). By setting these images free she was able to also release her own hitherto inhibited and restricted self.

After the experience of Daydream 5, she associated the encounter with the dragon in its watery cave in some way with the inability of a baby (herself) to *verbalise* its emotions and concluded that it is not always easy for an adult to do so either, conclusions which she based on her own life. She also said that she felt more confident and able to make her way in life. Her own wording "I feel that I have put out the dragon's fire permanently" and it poses "no longer any threat to me" sums up very well her increased ability to face life in a mature way.

In the sixth daydream, she was surprised that her "Prince Charming" turned out to be the old family doctor, long ago dead, whom she had equated unconsciously as a parental model, her *father-figure.* Her real father had left her mother when Anna was a tiny baby so she had never really known him. In her relationships with men most of her life she had been very immature, sexually inhibited, possibly seeking the father-figure she had needed because she had tended always to look for friendly relationships with much older men. As Anna's self-awareness increased, besides changing her career in favour of a caring profession in nursing, it was interesting that she not only met and formed a close relationship with a man of her own age but her former inhibitions disappeared and she was able to enjoy a fully mature sexual relationship.

Barbara (Case Ref: C.133)

This client's earlier years were dominated by her mother so that she tended to compensate for this by withdrawal into her own phantasy world. As a teenager she enjoyed her father's company and his gentle and kindly approach to life. His presence and support by "just being there" had provided a sort of shield against the real world, which she feared. Although she had married and had two children she had still needed the support of her father's presence. His death, besides shattering her phantasy world of ideals, created a void or vacuum and filled her with a despair for there had seemed to be no future in life. She recognised that the faceless "higher being" was very much associated with her inability to come to terms with her spiritual self and that she had unconsciously treated her father as providing the answers she had needed. She felt that her late father's mediation on her behalf in the fourth directed daydream had in some way resolved the problem and reassured her. She knew that she really loved her husband and this had been evidenced by his being the fairy tale prince who awakened her. However, her attitude to society had been one of facing it with a flippant attitude because in reality she feared it. Then, with the responsibilities of married life and motherhood she had thought that a more mature attitude would be expected of her. Thus, having discarded the defence of flippancy with nothing to replace it, her agoraphobic withdrawal became her only way out.

With the awakening confidence, which came from her understanding of herself, she made rapid improvement, overcoming the condition of agoraphobia. Indeed, at the conclusion of therapy she was able to go away on holiday with her family touring the countryside. She and her husband sent me a delightful post-card from one of the places at which they stayed which simply read:

"Thank you for being who you are! Hope, we're sure, you will enjoy yourself too!" (a reference to the fact that I was also going on holiday later that month).

Eleanor (Case Ref: F.19)

The *Owgle,* in Daydream 2, she saw as representing her own *inner* strength and wisdom, which had to be employed in her encounter with the blackish-green monster with twelve heads. The porpoise that guided her through the weeds to the monster's grotto she interpreted as her own *intuition.* By confronting the monster with her own powers she caused eleven of its heads to become lost, while the last head was transformed into a brighter green and less fearsome. This she interpreted as being her determination to confront her inner fears for by so doing they lost their power over her. She felt that something still remained which she needed to overcome (the twelfth head). The old book she saw as being the Akashic Records to which her greater mystical awareness was giving her access whilst the pressed flowers inside these records she saw as aspects of her late husband's influences on her own life. Their symbolism, she thought, was particularly significant. She confided that she had, at first been shocked to discover that her late husband was a transvestite, which she had initially equated to effeminate (pansy) behaviour but later, through her study of Jung, was able to accept as her late husband's way of coming to terms with his anima or feminine side. She confessed that it in no way affected his sexual capabilities, which she described as being exceptional and which she could not forget (symbolised by the *forget-me-knot*). The clover, the symbol of luck, was representative to her of how fortunate she had been to share the experiences she had with him which had helped her own *mystical evolvement* enormously.

When the monster was turned into the young man "physically most attractive" she felt that she had been fearful that she would never find her male counterpart in real life. The inner assurance that "he will always be there" she was convinced related to her *animus* and this she felt was borne out by the Angel she meets "with male appearance but (who is) actually androgynous". The beautiful description of "the effervescence from my chalice merges with the Angel's own light into a perfect blending" can but refer to the *alchemical wedding.*

In the session following Daydream 3 she had several cognitions about the ANIMUS and the female child within her. She said that she had experienced an inner awakening and her original problems no longer seemed to have importance because she recognised them as being of the outer or material world. She said that after writing up the Daydream she had meditated upon it and had felt strongly that she had experienced the *inner* marriage and the ecstasy of the *spiritual* orgasm.

So far as aspects of the dream itself were concerned she explained that when mounting one of the four reddish-black horses, she felt that somehow she was confronting *herself.* This was also reinforced too by her understanding of her turbulent feeling, strong *resistance* and then realising that she was "... sensing the thrill of power", real spiritual power. Even before encountering the father image she knew instinctively that his power would be ineffectual against that of her own *integrated* powers. She explained that the sorcerer's eyes were his strongest weapon because they resembled Marty Feldman's eyes, which she said had always disturbed her, striking a chord of fear within her, the fear of madness. The petrified "captives" she identified as being fears within herself but which she knew she was capable of overcoming with the *gold star* (the achievement of the spiritual crown) from the horse's mane; the horse being an aspect of herself.

Following Daydream 4, she told me that the old woman in charge of the horses, with her gnarled hands and wrinkled face and classical witch-like appearance, had been like a woman she once saw when she was out with her daughter. At that time the encounter had upset her but until the Daydream she had not realised why, or rather had not faced up to *why.* She realised that the woman represented the decay of the physical, outer appearance. Like the Witch-Queen in the story *Snow-White and the Seven Dwarfs* who through her obsession with her outer appearance, used her magical powers to transform herself from the beautiful, haughty, demanding woman into a harridan, Eleanor realised that she, too, had been afraid of losing her own youthful looks and although the outer worldly appearances are transitory, illusory, they nevertheless had affected her, rather as they had also affected her own mother. In this respect she was aware that her mother's influence on her life had been far more powerful than that of her father.

Daydream 5 was interesting since Eleanor was dressed like the fool in the tarot and represented more of the masculine figure (the ANIMUS) with which she was now quite familiar. Her overcoming of the dragon was, in her own words, easy because of her spiritual awakening which put the dragon (societal constraints) in its true perspective. The materialisation of the sword (male) in her left hand (female) and the chalice (female) in her right hand (male) had indicated the awakened powers she now possessed and against which society's constraints were ineffective. Again, the blossoming of the desert is further symbolism of her triumph in this respect.

In the final Daydream, Pegasus, the white horse helps her to reach the castle and therein she is in conflict with the beast, the devil himself. This daydream was a very profound one indeed for Eleanor and one for which she could find no easy translation because it represented an *inner* experience.

There were six further sessions with Eleanor following the Daydreams during which time she reported that she had met in real life a man who strikingly resembled her Viking Prince! The two of them were married fourteen months later.

Anita (Case Ref: G.93)

In the first Daydream, the vessel or chalice she was given was described as being "shiny, white porcelain ... which (she) kept in a protective bag around her waist". She recognised that she had been too aware of her fragility and had become over-protective towards herself, the cause of her anxiety and agoraphobia. In her second Daydream (Chapter 6), Anita's "monster" or fear turned out to be a teddy-bear which she recognised as being symbolic of her father, a somewhat sad figure who, like herself, had been dominated by her mother and consequently had "missed out in life".

The third and fourth Daydreams were interesting inasmuch as she had already comes to terms with her parents in the previous Daydream. In the third Daydream she changed the Sorcerer's book of spells into a Bible and then gave him a pair of sunglasses so that he could "come out into the sunlight" with her. She interpreted this as meaning that her father, a quiet man who appeared to her to be struggling with religion and certainly having little understanding of mysticism, had first to be introduced to the *orthodox* aspects rather as she herself had done, before he could be introduced to the brighter light. She told me that she bore her father no animosity as she believed him to be both loving and thoughtful when not pre-occupied! In Daydream 4, the Witch, her mother, threw a snake at her feet that Anita overcame with a stone from her vessel, which she threw onto it whereupon "it shrivelled up". In discussion, at the next session, Anita translated the symbolism as meaning that her mother no longer had any power over her and she was able to discuss freely their real-life relationship, the barrier between them to which she felt they had both contributed. Having come to terms with it, she seemed much more together as a person. In fact, she was able to discuss her whole family quite frankly—father, mother and grandparents and whilst feeling disapproval at times confessed that she had often acted in a similar manner to them!

The fifth Daydream was her unique way of coming to terms with society's constraints. She had, in the past, been affected by other people's opinions of her and the judgement which society *en masse* made. She tried in her Daydream to "rise above it" by demonstrating her own light and then became aware that the dragon was not *so big* after all! Its metamorphosis into a golden dragon was accomplished by disappearing inside itself and sprouting large wings. It relied on another for generating its power, which she interpreted as being upon those, like her, who collectively made up society and together instituted its laws and constraints. She believed that the majority of those who make up society, however, are motivated by outer, material, considerations rather than from inner, spiritual motivation. Having eventually 'slain the dragon', after she had accepted that there was no way she could transform it, she met the child within herself who had been too timid to try and thus became more mature in her attitude to society. On discussing the fifth daydream she went through an incredible amount of losses in her life ... the loss of various friends who gave up training in nursing, the deaths of both her grandparents, the loss of her first husband who left her for another woman, her own loss of dignity, the loss of a relative who was a murder victim, the loss of her favourite uncle, etc. Most of these recalls of losses in her life were accompanied by emotional releases.

When discussing the sixth and final Daydream with her she said that the Beast had been indecisive and she believed represented the negative side of her father. The servant-head she had encountered she said had "kept hanging about" in her memory and she had identified her as being her mother. She then recalled that her mother had once made a very prolonged visit to her home and had occupied the spare room which was adjacent to her bedroom and throughout her mother's stay Anita had felt so inhibited that she had been unable to have any normal marital relationship with her husband.

Following the Daydreams, and although feeling much better in herself to the point of once again being able to accompany her husband and family on walks in the town and the countryside, she decided to continue in therapy, during the sessions of which there was a great deal of abreaction, resulting from incidents during her childhood; incidents which included two operations after being taken to the hospital and left there by her father on both occasions, and bullying at school.

Rita (Case Ref: M.37)

This was the client whose heart had stopped beating during a severe asthma attack and who was resuscitated by a colleague; since when she had suffered depression and other distressing symptoms. Nevertheless, it will be seen from Daydream one that her description of her chalice (herself) and its content was good.

Her ascent of the mountain, representing her higher self, necessitated her going through water, her emotions, and even going across to "the other side" to attain the loftiest peak. She saw this as very symbolic of her own death (or near-death) experience. Because of her earlier religious upbringing the ascent beyond the mountain was full of Christian symbolism. Her descent in the second Daydream did not frighten her at all and indicated to her that there were no *major* difficulties that were beyond her ability to resolve. The transformation of the monster into a fairy prince, fairy godmother and a unicorn, with the unicorn in dominance, Rita believed all these to be aspects of her deeper consciousness, her inner world, and were meaningful to her although she could not interpret them fully. Although she had taken nothing from the experience "in the *physical* sense", she did take with her the "sound of bells". She interpreted this as being a spiritual awakening, that her experiences had indeed rung the inner bell of understanding.

It is not the purpose of the therapist to translate or evaluate his client's dream symbols. As Jung admits in *Man and his symbols* "I have made it a rule to remind myself that I can never understand somebody else's dream well enough to interpret it". Indeed, the role of the therapist is one of encouraging his client to explore the content of a dream with the utmost thoroughness, never evaluating its symbolism for the client. However, Jung says that "... many symbols, among them the most important, are not *individual* but *collective*. These are chiefly religious images". He adds: "... their origin is so far buried in the mystery of the past that they *seem* to have no human source ... they are, in fact, 'collective representations' emanating from primeval dreams and creative fantasies. As such, these images are involuntary spontaneous manifestations and by no means intentional inventions."

Following Daydream 3, she appraised her description of the wizard or sorcerer as being like "an acorn". To her, this was the relationship with her father, which had not been developed but had the potential there. just as the acorn held within it the potential of becoming the mighty oak tree. She translated the unevenness of the ground as being uncertainty in her relationship with him during her earlier years, while the bats which were flying about and singing she thought were symbolic of freedom through *flight*, away from situations she had been unable to face during childhood but which by escaping had given her a temporary illusion of happiness. There is "light from above" she equated to her increased illumination or understanding of herself. She interpreted the "acrid, yet somehow pleasant smell" of the fire as being symbolic of the reconciliation of opposites within her own personality and psyche. The fact that she initially took a *sideways* rather than a *direct* look at her paternal archetype in the Daydream, symbolised to her how she had viewed her father in real life. The reptile on the windowsill was related to when she was ill in hospital in Greece and had experienced a dream involving a lizard and had, in that dream, become a symbol of a cry for help. She recognised the paternal archetype dressed like a monk and being a friend, or teacher as her own father who was a Theosophist. Her jump into the blue light she interpreted as being symbolic of creating a neural path to her own healing and realised that her subsequent feeling of being full of energy had something to do with the previously misplaced energy of "shaking" now being available to her in a more positive form. The session following her third daydream showed a marked improvement in her condition, not only in the absence of the former shaking but also in the recovery of her sense of balance.

Daydream four she recognised as being to do with the archetypal mother but believed that the incident with Henry VIII was extremely profound and related to her own near death and recovery. She told me that the whole scenario had recaptured something of a former life around the 1500's. She also said that the episode in the tunnel when she was trying to leave the room of the Sorceress, was symbolic of her own birth and she had felt this whilst living the episode in the Daydream. She interpreted the colours as being indicative of her own spiritual progress, as indeed was the transformation of the desert in the following Daydream five and the maturing of the child within to spiritual maturity, culminating in the metamorphosis or transformation when the chalice becomes enveloped into a huge butterfly and bathed in blue light.

The final Daydream she believed, similarly, to be an *initiation* full of mystical symbolism: the growing up of the young man into maturity (the ANIMUS), the reconciliation of this aspect of herself with her female image and the rose-garden, typical of what mystics term the Alchemical Wedding. The Chalice being described as almost weightless and like the colour of lightning "as if (at last) it has its own life ..."

This terminated her sessions but some time later she wrote to me:

"As to my health I'm told I look wonderful!" It seems that the conditions she had consulted me about when she first came to therapy had all cleared or improved except for the arthritic pain which she described as being "... more slow to respond but I think it is ...!"

She had subsequent treatment from a chiropractor which proved most beneficial and he, in turn, referred her to a medical colleague who carried out tests for food intolerances from which it was discovered that she was intolerant of potatoes, tomatoes, sugar, soya, curry, tea and alcohol.

Fairly recently this former client approached me to ask if I would be prepared to accept a male friend of hers as a client but as I had then retired from practice I referred them to the National Council of Psychotherapists who put them in touch with one of my colleagues who, according to Rita, "proved to be most helpful, clearing out his 'rubbish' rapidly after only two sessions!"

Sylvia (Case Ref: M.164)

This was the client who had been raped at knifepoint. It will be obvious from Daydreams one and two that considerable resistance had to be overcome, although Sylvia eventually succeeded in climbing the mountain and the stairway beyond. In the second Daydream her monster was Godzilla whom she described as "the *opposite* to King Kong and Kong defeated it", later describing Kong "as the beast who loved the woman". Her *greatest* fear seemed to be of Lisa, formerly her boy-friend's dog , into which the monster changed when she touched it for the second time with her chalice. She was not afraid of Lisa *but what Lisa represented* to her. Her description of the animal: "... it is a bitch (female) but aggressive and can tackle other dogs (males) fearlessly". She realised that she had been angry with herself for a very long time for not being brave enough to stand up to her attacker with "death before dishonour" and saw Lisa as a reminder of her own fears. One session was spent in discussing this with her at the conclusion of which she forgave herself and accepted the reality that she had lived to tell the tale, as it were, and at twenty-six years of age had her life in front of her.

Following Daydream 3, in which she encounters many representative images of the males in her life, she had a massive emotional release whilst at the cinema with her boy friend, sobbing uncontrollably, after which she slept and felt fine when she awoke. Subsequently, throughout the following week she was less work conscious, treating life in a much more relaxed fashion and getting on well with the girls she supervised.

In her fourth Daydream, Sylvia had a difficult session and it will be obvious from her statements that her relationship with her mother proved difficult and yet she felt that it was a situation from which there had been no escape for her. She obviously had been very much under her mother's influence. During the session the week following the Daydream she described an incident when she was seven years of age where she was at play with some girl friends of her own age. Their game was rather like a play and involved dressing up in some old clothing of adult style. Sylvia, was directing the play. It seems that her mother had interrupted the game at a point where one of the participants was being tied to a post. Her mother hid the clothes afterwards and refused to explain why she had done so.

Sylvia told me during this session that although she had been frigid ever since being raped, since undertaking the Daydreams she had had several nocturnal dreams of a sexual nature during which she had experienced orgasm.

Daydream five proved interesting to her because she felt that although she had worked through many of her inner fears and was on the road to recovery after the traumatic real-life experience she had endured, she still tended to accept things fatalistically rather than taking control over situations. Yet she felt that her experiences in the Daydream were telling her to take life more light-heartedly and that somehow she felt within herself that she was on course.

Daydream six accomplished a great deal for her, setting her free from the problem she had suffered. One or two further sessions were undertaken but she told me that she felt fine. She volunteered for hypnosis to curb her over-eating and rapidly began to return to her normal weight. She married her boy friend a year later and as he had obtained well-paid employment in Scotland, she resigned her job and the couple moved home. She told me at the conclusion of her hypnotherapy sessions that whenever she found herself in tension in any situation she calmed herself by visualising a lovely scene from the first daydream.

Michaela (Case Ref: O.45)

The conclusion of the first Daydream brought about a complete change in this client's attitude. She said that it was very helpful to her that her late grandfather, a kind and gentle man, appeared on the Stairway beyond the mountaintop as she had always trusted him and looked up to him. In the second Daydream the monster turned out to be her boy friend whom she loved. This was something of a surprise at first but after she had given this some thought she decided that her greatest fear was not really *him* but rather the advances that he made towards her and to which she was unable to respond. This being due to a most unpleasant incident that had happened to her when she was thirteen years old. She said that she had been pushed into a hedge and raped by three gypsies, one of whom was married with a baby. It seems that he was the brother of a girl whom she had befriended at school. She had been a virgin before the rape and afterwards she said that she felt unclean and degraded and was afraid to tell her family what had happened to her. It was an incident of such horror to her that over the years since then she had suffered various mental disturbances including *anorexia nervosa*.

Following Daydream three she said that the man at the cottage seemed to her to be like her father but yet he didn't resemble him physically at all. It was interesting that following her birth, Michaela was left with her grandparents much of the time as they occupied the house next door-but-one to that of her parents. She thought that probably her late grandfather had assumed the role of father to her. The fourth Daydream was very interesting inasmuch as when she touched the witch it had the effect of melting her into a pool. The description of the witch (old, fat and short) and that of her captives (skinny and starving) seemed to bring about some inner understanding, which she was unable to verbalise. The fact that "the woman at the cottage who looks like my mother" had laughed in disbelief when Michaela had told her that she had completed her mission she equated to her mother's sceptical attitude which to some degree she had shared, finding it difficult to believe that Desoille's

Daydreams could make such a profound change in her life. What is more important is that at the conclusion of these daydreams there had been such a change for the better that her mother had recognised it and telephoned me to say how pleased she was with her daughter's progress, Michaela having become fitter, more confident, was eating properly and regaining weight. What better testimony to Desoille's method but this young lady's words: "I feel so confident somehow!"

The fifth Daydream was not difficult for her and she felt that this was because she had an inner strength that she had lacked before and was able to carry this with her in her day-to-day living. No longer did she feel afraid of Society or its judgements and prejudices. She was obviously going through the inner awakening, the Self-realisation of which Roberto Assagioli speaks in *Self-Realisation and Psychological Disturbances.*

The sixth Daydream followed the normal pattern with her prince, her boy friend, Mark, arousing her from her sleep. Two months after the conclusion of therapy, Michaela telephoned me (on Christmas Eve) to advise me that she had just become engaged to Mark. The following year she gave up her factory work to undertake work in child-care.

Beryl (Case Ref: W.154)

Her interpretation of her first attempt at ascending the mountain and the stairway beyond was that she had experienced difficulty in facing her *real self.* The gaping hole, which appeared in the stairway, she thought to be symbolic of the gap in her own evolution. This, she explained, needed subsequent resting-time to recover her strength, this being symbolic of the time needed to recuperate from a horrendous motor accident in which she was involved, it being nothing short of a miracle that she survived, and to allow her to readjust after her disappointing marriage. After eventually crossing a platform to bridge the gap, she was confronted by a statue of Christ, which she identified as representing her inability to reconcile her deeper religious feelings with the dogma of orthodoxy: "*the Christ was a statue, not a Spirit*".

In her second attempt at this Daydream, the living Being dressed in a white robe (purity) who descended to meet her with arms outstretched, she believed to be symbolic of coming to terms with her higher Self. The chalice, "highly coloured, classically shaped and of Indian brass" she saw as being the outer appearance with which she confronted the world.

In the second Daydream her descent into the ocean, (symbolic of descending into the depths of one's deeper emotions and confronting one's more suppressed characteristics), was *with her eyes closed.* She saw this as meaning that she was *afraid* of what she might discover in the depths of her own being! The shutter across the entrance to the grotto she believed to be an attempt to hide or evade something that lay beyond. This was a classical illustration of *resistance* for she became out of breath and had to return to the surface for air and rest. On my insistence that after resting she should make a second attempt, there was again resistance when she grasped hold of the shutter instead of entering the cave or grotto. She recognised that "the man dressed in black" (her *animus*) was the darker side of her own nature. When she touched him with the Chalice she had a cognition that he was there to help her and that *she* was the monster.

This was a real breakthrough for Beryl. She said that all her life she had acted out the role of the helpless female, the innocent little girl needing protection from the wicked world. The second Daydream had given her recognition that each and every one of us has to balance the male and female within ourselves, the positive and the negative, the animus and anima. In Beryl's case the real *monster* was no longer the repressed masculine side of her nature but the too heavily emphasised female role under which she had hidden. Beyond, the cave, was like her own house, which contained all her real fears: old age, death, a black hole with seemingly no way out. She said that when I had told her to touch herself with the chalice, she had immediately become two people, one good, the other evil. Her victory over the evil one she saw as symbolic of the inherent power of control over our baser, lower instincts. The evil had melted away and all that remained was a black cloak and stick, the outer appearance, as it were. This also gave her, it seems, a profound recognition that the real self, the good within, survives beyond the physical death. The discussions with her, which followed on from the actual session of the second Daydream, embraced a further two sessions. In these she told me that she had led a rather sheltered childhood and shortly after the deaths within a very short time of both her parents, she met and married her present husband anticipating that wedded life would be rather like the fairy-tale "happily ever after" situation. However, her husband was actually homosexual and had used the marriage as a cover of respectability for the benefit of his business career. Thus, she had been forced to live a lie whenever they entertained her husband's business colleagues. When the full horror of what she had let herself in for dawned on her she began suffering migrainous headaches and then panic attacks. These had steadily got worse, becoming much more frequent over the years. Then, two years before consulting me, she was involved in a serious car crash and had to be cut free from her wrecked car. She suffered severe injuries in this accident including a fractured skull, fractured limbs and severe lacerations to her face, chest and arms. She was rushed to hospital and during the initial part of her stay in hospital she was unconscious. When she recovered from the coma, she suffered severe depression and for many months was under the care of a psychiatrist who sedated her with psychiatric drugs and on whose instructions she underwent a series of six ECT sessions (electric shock therapy).

In the final part of the second Daydream, she was " . . . met by a Higher Being, adorned in a pure white cloak and having a fire in front of him" and the transformation of her chalice into a sword shaped like a cross with the blade being of finest silver and the hilt of purest gold (with) Jesus being upon its hilt. At the beginning of the third Daydream she insisted on going back up the stairway to meet the Higher Being again. Her interpretation of the third Daydream was given in Chapter 7.

Resistance was encountered in Daydream 4 and following its discussion Beryl told me that she had experienced some guilt feelings. These had been caused by her late mother's religious and somewhat stoical acceptance of her father in spite of his alcohol problem. Many times, of course, her mother's patience had been taxed to the limit and she had become very angry although Beryl as a young child failed to understand *why* and had felt some sympathy for her father. Over the years the affect of her unhappy marriage had taken its toll in her mother's increasingly haggard appearance. Beryl now was looking at her own imperfect marriage and while one part of her wanted to leave her husband, another part identified with her mother's life and that conditioning was telling her that it was sinful to even think of leaving and in any case to do so would mean losing her home and the need, like her mother, "to have *some* company". This had brought about deeper feelings of guilt when she had agreed that the doctors should withdraw the life-support machine and that she might have deprived her mother of a little of her father's presence by so doing. Following the write-up and subsequent discussion of the fourth Daydream she faced up to her fears and why she had felt so unhappy for so long. She realised that she did not *have* to leave or stay with her husband but whatever course she eventually took she would have weighed up and done what she *wanted* to do.

Following the fifth Daydream she explained that she no longer felt any fear of Society or the constraints that it had once imposed upon her. Her offer to make friends with the dragon if it ceased to behave badly she felt meant that she was prepared to take part in Society provided it accepted her on her own terms. In her real life situation she had the opportunity of leaving her husband and going away with another man but could not make up her mind whether to do this or stay with her husband. Her meeting with the Arab on the black horse who asked her to "go the other way with him" was the very opposite of the things in her life and symbolised her Animus. This masculine side of her being she saw as representing a tempter, trying to lure her away from her spiritual path. On the mountain she first meets a pleasant looking man with dark curly hair who was waiting for her, knowing that she would come back. The Arab was waiting on the peak of the mountain but she passed him by and climbed higher to meet the Christ who welcomes her with outstretched arms. By offering the chalice (herself) to Him she is rewarded by a replacement golden cup with a crown on top, which she thought symbolised her "second birth". On the far side of the mountain she meets both the Arab and "the other man" and she had to make a choice. This was the parallel in her life with her husband and the need to have a warm, loving relationship. The Arab and she ascend together (the marriage of opposites). She looked down as if it were the last time she will see that part of her - the separate female attributes. She believed herself to have become an integrated and spiritually mature being.

The final Daydream was really one of her reaching sexual maturity and recognising that although she was highly motivated spiritually, she had to accept that she was a person who enjoyed sensual pleasure too. The Lion she recognised as representing aspects of both her husband and her late father, while the Panther symbolised the "other man" in her life over whom she believed she could exercise control and which, therefore, did not constitute a threat. The *real* beast, however, had the *body* of a man but the *head* of the Lion and this was her husband. He symbolised the father figure on whom she had become dependent.

Subsequent sessions with her were used to help her overcome the smoking habit and discuss other aspects in her life. Her health improved steadily throughout therapy. On her final consultation she said that there were things she still had to work through but she felt better equipped to do it.

Colin (Case Ref: L.70)

In his first Daydream the ascent of the mountain and then the golden stairway of sunlight were accomplished and the subsequent meeting with "Pure Light" filled Colin with much needed optimism and self-confidence. The sword he was given showed that his self-image had improved immensely.

In the session following his second Daydream, we saw that Colin's greatest fear was that of becoming just an ordinary man, which he saw as some sort of failure in life.

Following Daydream 3, discussions with Colin indicated that his relationship with his mother had its ups and downs; at times he had the upper hand but more frequently she had it! However, he said that he was really fond of his mother and imagined that most of his peers had similar relationships with their mothers. He assured me that although he was very fond of his mother he was not suffering a mother-fixation problem! He admitted that at times he had felt dominated by her and thought this was the reason she was able to take the sword away from him at one point in the dream. His being able to retrieve it while the sorceress was occupied by the grey horse he could not understand but thought that it might possibly have had some connection with his arguing skills which frequently made his opponent forget the main point of an argument. He said that arguments with his parents were no exception.

Daydream 4 had to be run through twice. On the first attempt the Sorcerer's face changed to that of Colin's father who was armed with a sword just like his! At first Colin found it difficult to accept that he had any similarity in appearance or in personality to his father. He saw his father as being many things - a jester, a warrior, an animal at times and cunning. He felt threatened by his father in real life and was on his guard. The ensuing battle in the Daydream ended in his piercing him "clean through the chest" but this was most distressing to Colin as he did not really wish his father harm. What he did was not commensurate with the gentler, feminine side of his nature, his *anima* that he had not yet recognised as being a part of his personality; hence the pure white wedding gown but black face. The second attempt was successful inasmuch as Colin was able to resist his father's attempts to dominate him yet at the same time being able to absorb the more positive aspects of his father's parental guidance. Following these Daydreams Colin's attitude to his real-life situation began to improve; first in his relationship with his parents and then in his contact with others.

Following the fifth Daydream, he made some astute interpretations of what had taken place. He explained that the barren desert, with hot air and sand blowing in it, was typical of modern society which too often was barren of real ideas for reform, frequently spouted a lot of hypocritical hot air and frequently possessed a sting like grains of sand in the wind. He said that the restraints of society are often very empty, founded on prejudices and had no real substance and vibrancy. The monk going about his simple task who told him where the dragon could be found represented to Colin the monastic life, apart from society and with which he felt some affinity; not for itself but because it was free of the generalities and uniformities of society. He said that the dragon was devouring someone when he first entered its cave. He exclaimed "Quite literally, society can do that!" After his encounter with the dragon he felt that society could be changed, the constraints imposed are by certain sections of the community but are not necessarily the views of all. The subsequent confrontation with the villagers was a real awakening for Colin. He no longer condemned society as being thoroughly bad but rather felt that some of its constraints were imposed for the good of society as a whole while others are not. He said that he also recognised that there is some good in all and that he hoped during his life, "to help create better understanding and peace". He was also aware that it is possible to have one's personality tainted by its encounters with society and its constraints.

The final Daydream showed that this young man was moving rapidly towards a genuine emotional maturity. Throughout the daydreams, with the exception of his first attempt at the third one, he had the ability to keep his wits in the face of embarrassing and dangerous situations, was able to examine them realistically and to respond with action which took into accounts the rights of others as well as his own interests, as was evidenced by his generosity, or tendency towards compassion in his confrontations with his adversaries. These are behavioural ideals; they are also essential if a person is to live in harmony with his fellows.

He wrote to me from college fifteen months after completion of therapy to let me know that he was doing well at the subjects he had chosen and had been very busy on two projects, one of which was on conservation and the recycling of waste and had actually given a talk on the subject, admitting that he felt nervous at first but rapidly warmed to his subject and was sorry when he came to the end of his talk!

Carl (Case Ref: M.130)

We saw in the first Daydream that this client was given *two* swords, one straight and the other curved and that he felt he was being asked to make a choice. This might have indicated some duality of being either in character, that is, straightforwardness versus deviousness, but I did not think so. I thought it far more likely that he was attempting to reconcile two polarities within himself, or, to put it another way to come to terms with the feminine side of his nature, the *anima.* In the second Daydream he pierced the monster with the straight sword to subdue it but when he had to confront it again on the second occasion, revealing his greatest fear, he used the curved sword, whereupon it turned into a mermaid. He interpreted this as being symbolic because of his difficulty in forming any lasting relationship with a woman.

In my case notes at the time I wrote the following observation: "It is very clear that there are two diametrically opposed attributes within the one being, the *positive* masculine attribute and the *negative* feminine attribute. All clients are seeking to balance these aspects within themselves; whether they recognise it or not on the purely analytical or mental level is immaterial; when it *is* accomplished they are provided then with far greater illumination and in this respect resembles the coming together of the positive and negative electrical currents, providing light and warmth".

In this case, the Higher Being met was Jesus ... who symbolised the highest possible goal of perfection to one who was brought up in the Christian tradition. The "monster" on the other hand was the snake or serpent (who tempted Eve and caused Adam's fall from Grace).

In his next session I asked Carl: "What does the mermaid represent?" To which he replied: "It is a creature, half woman, half fish".

"Yes, but what do you *fear*?"

"I feared the monster, the snake".

"Yet you faced it and eventually changed it into the mermaid".

This seemed to please him. I explained that the basic purpose of the second Daydream is to discover what is going on in the *depths* of your being. What painful feelings are capable of upsetting you. And less obvious is the implication *is there scope for change?*

He thought about this for a time and then told me: "Perhaps changing the snake into a mermaid shows that there is".

I agreed that this was so, for if a client is unable to cause that change in the Daydream he will most likely be unable to do so in his real life situation. The fact that he had caused a change from monster to mermaid indicated that he is *fully capable* of bringing about changes in his real life situation.

At this point he explained that in build he was much slighter than that of most of the other lorry drivers and as he favoured growing his hair long the others called him "gay". This had worried him because he was thirty-one and had failed to have a lasting relationship with a woman. At first, he had dismissed this as being due to the vagaries of his working hours but after being taunted by the other drivers he began to worry as to whether he might actually be homosexual, deep down. When I told him about the *anima* and the *animus* he thought that it was possible that the mermaid, representing only half a woman, might have symbolised a fear of the feminine side of his own nature but he thought it much more likely that his real fear was that he would not have a woman at all, a *full*-time female partner or wife, to make his life complete or fulfilled. He was very fascinated by Carl G. Jung at this point and asked me to recommend some of his writings, which he decided he would study in his spare time.

After the third Daydream, coming to terms with the parent of the opposite sex, there was considerable improvement in his attitude to life. When he knew the purpose of the Daydream he said that his own experiences he had interpreted as follows:

The brambles on the mountain equated to minor irritations while the attack by the black dog, which gripped his arm, equated to the restriction he had sometimes felt at home which had tended to impede his freedom. The bear was larger than the dog so he thought this possibly had symbolised an increased threat of interference in his life that he had fought off with the curved sword or the feminine side of his nature. When asked whether he could clarify this, he told me that his intuition was responsible for his going for the long-distance lorry-driving job *because* it involved absences from home. The male knight on the white horse who told him not to enter the cave, therefore not to confront his mother, was some part of his nature, which did not want a confrontation. To him, the knight stood for male chivalry. The horse ridden by the knight he took to be a symbol of life, of freedom. In like manner the bats also symbolised release in some way. The witch's cauldron he believed to be symbolic of her potential power *over him* but which he decisively rejected. He saw the little devils with pitchforks as niggling incidents which had threatened his independence but which he faced up to squarely and honestly by using the straight sword. Standing up also to the witch's futile attacks, following which she crumpled up, was symbolic to him of his being capable of detaching himself from her influence.

In the fourth Daydream the black dog actually bit his hand and jokingly he remarked that perhaps the father-figure's bite was worse than his bark; that is, more capable of affecting him than the mother influences. He also felt that in some way it symbolised his severance of the former parental hold over him. The elephant symbolised his own father's nature, that of being a plodder, albeit with a long memory! The witch flying past on her broomstick symbolised his mother's influence *over* both him and his father. The wizard's cave being jewelled he thought were his father's cardinal qualities, which he admired. He believed that his request for the *key* was a recognition that the father figure could help him. This was symbolised too by the clear *direction* he was given which, by following, led him to the box that could be opened by the key. It was the box that was valuable (he handed back the key) because it contained the ring that would give him the maiden. I told Carl that Jung had regarded the ring or circle as being the symbol of the Self, the Psyche (*Man and His Symbols,* pp 240 - 249) and Carl felt that this was so in his dream. The ring, which he intuitively felt to be within the box, he considered to be an excellent description of the SELF within the body. The rest of the session was spent in discussing the *anima* at the conclusion of which Carl was prepared to accept, following his study of Jung's writings, that for want of a better explanation this was most likely what the maiden in the dream symbolised to him.

The early difficulties with the barbed wire fence in the fifth Daydream he found to be very symbolic of his earlier years when he was aware of the barrier that seemed to exist between himself and the other children at school. He recalled an incident when he had been taken to nursery school by his mother but when she had attempted to leave him there he had gone into a state of near hysteria and had to be taken home. The slippery sands were like the changing sands of time, which epitomised his own attempts to come to terms with society. The oasis which he found but where he was quite alone he interpreted as being his attempts at escapism. He told me that as far back as he could remember he had had a real fondness for all animal life which taken in its positive aspect was fine but he had asked himself whether in its more negative aspect he trusted animals more than humans. He felt that his first approach to the dragon's cave was again symbolic of his own life in which he had followed no proper plan but rather taking things as life handed them out. He decided that in his own life in future he would be different and seek a much more purposeful plan. The initial use of the curved sword he thought might be his earlier negative or furtive approach and that going for the dragon's eyes was so the dragon (society) would no longer be able to see his weaknesses and imperfections. By changing to the straight sword and going for the dragon's throat he believed was symbolically the overcoming of the vociferous and condemning voice of society and its ability to swallow him up. He equated this to his developing consciousness and maturity. The whole encounter had not left him unscathed as evidenced by the cuts on his arms. He also saw the need to maintain an oasis in his real life where he could withdraw at times, not in escapism but more to recharge himself. He saw the jewels that he removed from the dragon's cave as being the treasures of knowledge and with their acquisition came greater responsibility. He had no difficulty in identifying the young woman as his *anima* on this occasion. He mentioned that handing over the jewels to the old man, the higher aspect of himself, as proof of his victory over the dragon was recognition that his newly discovered wisdom and power could easily be employed in bringing him material security but their real worth was in his own development. This he saw as being similar in some way to the temptations to which Jesus was subjected.

The final Daydream was typically Jungian, he thought, with the knight, big-framed and armed with a sword and an axe, constituting a threat to his personal "battle for deliverance"! Whilst this may well have constituted the realisation of the shadow (Jung's *Man and his Symbols* pp. 93, 168), to quote Jung: "In some aspects the shadow can also consist of collective factors that stem from a source outside the individual's personal life". The very build of the knight and his constituting a threat was not far removed from the real-life situation, which Carl had constantly faced in his work situation, epitomised by the taunts and innuendoes made by his fellow drivers that had made him doubt his own masculinity. The realisation of the shadow is an important step in life. It is not the complete unconscious personality but it does represent unknown or partially known attributes and qualities of the ego; aspects that mostly belong to "the personal sphere and that could just as well be conscious". In the Daydream the shadow invariably pops up as a person of the same sex as the client. Carl by this time had decided to change his employment and a few sessions later he concluded therapy having obtained employment to which he was much better suited intellectually and emotionally.

Warren (Case Ref: S.164)

From the accounts of his first two Daydreams it was evident that his life was dominated by his mother and that his greatest fear was that he would be incapable of a happy union with Jenny, his girl friend.

In his session following the third Daydream, he said he felt that he had already overcome the witch when he was able to ascend the 'impassable rocky outcrop' in the first Daydream that resembled his mother and I was inclined to agree with him. In the third Daydream he described the witch as representing no threat to him at all. The gnomes, which he released, he identified with his own earlier years and felt that he should have freed himself more from his mother's dominant attitude. He recognised that the witch was upset by his leaving her and felt this to be similar to the problem he might have to face if he married Jenny.

The fourth Daydream he saw the torch on his left side as representing his mother's influence in his appraisal of his father; that is, he had tended to view his father in the light of the impression conveyed to him by his mother. He saw the thick granite wall as something that had been built up over the years since his early childhood and which had prevented his getting close to his father. He told me that his father was considerably older than his mother and was somewhat weak and frail due to health problems. Warren respected his father's age but believed that his father's real personality had been somewhat stifled, there was much potential within the man although he did not make the most of it. Again, he did not like to turn his back on his father, that is, by leaving him if he were to marry Jenny.

The fifth Daydream was extremely interesting because although the theme is coming to terms with societal constraints, once again the witch dominates much of the action at the beginning. Warren was fully aware that his mother tended to care a great deal what people thought about her and her family. Her figure became smaller as he entered the hills, which he translated as meaning the more he evolved the less her influence over him became. However, his exteriorisation and being able to rise above all the restrictions he believed to be extremely symbolic and the part of himself which stood beside the witch he recognised was but a shell, an aspect of his former self, which he had since outgrown. He saw his path as being illumined, surrounded by the light of understanding, even the rising of the sun behind the hill heralded a symbolic new dawn for him. Even so, he was aware of the dominant mother influence, which still tried to hold him back, and decided that in his real-life situation he should adopt a different approach; head-on confrontation had not proved effective but a more subtle appeal to the higher motivation within his parents and society might. The desert "which now has vegetation springing up all around" he believed symbolised that the barren aspects of his own life had disappeared, to be replaced by new growth, new opportunities. There was a major emotional release during this Daydream.

The final Daydream was full of symbolism which took two sessions to unravel but its final interpretation to Warren's satisfaction, was as follows:-

"The fairy-tale castle I think was like my own immature view of life. The arena with the two men locked in combat was symbolic of the battle that had raged within myself and the combatants were aspects of myself. The Neanderthal man was the baser, instinctive part of myself, which was vulnerable, while the knight was the rational part of myself. The knight was originally armed with a trident and a net, both being used in water. The knight pushed the trident into the throat of the instinctive or crude man, thus attempting to silence him but the instinctive man has a "big fat red tongue and keeps lifting up his head and gasping". This indicated that the battle was ongoing and the instinctive man could not be silenced. The fact that the conflict was watched by monks convinced me that this was a typical combat between my higher and lower natures. There was no escape from this conflict, no evading it, it was something I had to face. There was a time when my rational side became dwarfed and that was when I turned to alcohol as a solution to my problems. However, this was just escapism and fortunately I now realise this, which is why my knight grew in stature again. Until the knight has the full use of *my* sword, *myself* it could not overcome the baser man by cutting off his head, his voice. The mace in the knight's hand represents his authority when the battle is finally won. The princess whom I awakened with a kiss was so beautiful and showed both affection and happiness. I wonder, is it possible to find such love as this in my life?

"I would like to think that there is in the form of Jenny but at times I worry that she might be like my mother and try to dominate me. Even my sword was like the wooden sword of a child and when I used such an immature approach it merely caused screaming and shouting. Yet by understanding her more, that is by accepting her feminine attributes, the real sword becomes available to me, which enabled me to come to terms with life on all levels, to come to terms with myself and my family. I believe that I can make it with Jenny, which is why she sat astride my white horse. I think that I had probably viewed settling down with her as being primitive like the igloo and the native hut, rather than the opportunity of sharing the beauty of life, which the Canadian waterfall symbolises to me. I believe that I should marry Jenny and that we can be happy."

Conclusion: In all, fifteen psychotherapy sessions had taken place. He had numerous emotional releases. He and Jenny did, in fact, marry. They spent their honeymoon in Bavaria from where Walt sent me a card. On his final consultation on return to England he said that he was most grateful for all the therapy sessions which had been responsible for his feeling "a thousand times better" and something which had been evident to and commented upon by everyone who knew him. He thought that of all the attempts made to overcome his psychological problems, the Desoille method was the first, which had really got to grips with them.

Stuart (Case Ref: T.68)

In the session following his first Daydream Stuart said that he had felt a definite emotional reaction when climbing the mountain and thought it probable that it had much to do with the employment he had undertaken since leaving College that year. He said that it was not the right occupation for him with his educational background and the chances of promotion to a higher managerial position would take years. He thought it probable that this might be the underlying reason for his suffering bouts of depression. From his description of the sword he was given by Jesus, it was evident that his self-image was good. It was interesting that he had to "force himself down" to what he described as being "too mundane below".

In the second Daydream he faced and subdued the black serpent, the cloak that covered his real fear, which turned out to be a girl. He enlists her support in recovering the treasure chest from the seabed. He admitted that he was not really afraid so much of the opposite sex but of finding himself in a marital situation which might turn out to be disastrous, like that of his parents. Even " . . . the girl's hair is blowing in the wind as we ascend but I feel no wind at all upon my face or hair" indicated to him that he thought of himself as being too serious, too up-tight, while most girls of his age seemed to be somewhat more carefree. When he opened the treasure chest at Jesus' command, many birds were released. He saw this as representing all the inhibitions that he had harboured for so long. This actually produced an emotional release for him.

The third Daydream, coming to terms with the parent of the opposite sex, produced obstacles in his way by way of roots and branches. The cave of the witch was situated on a slope between two gently sloping hills, which he later described as of a comforting, pleasant scene. When asked if it reminded him of anything he said that it was shaped rather like a woman's breast in appearance. When discussing this he told me that his mother had left his father when he was quite young and for some reason he had been left with his father. He said that he used to visit his mother as a boy and still did now that he was a man but that a sort of barrier had existed between them since she left him and this he equated to the invisible barrier, which he encountered in the cave of the witch. He said that both he and his mother were aware of the barrier between them caused by her deserting him but there was a sort of tacit understanding between them that this was a subject, which was never talked about. The fact that he walked into the cave backwards was, he felt, very symbolic. His sword hand was encumbered by his holding on to the wall and this he interpreted as meaning that his progress in life had been rendered more difficult by his mother's leaving him. The red glow *behind* her represented their past life together before she left and his presence seeming to kindle the fire he thought might be his having held on to the past and its happier associations. He felt that she had a very strong hold on him and that this was demonstrated in the Daydream when she took his sword and held on to it and he could only free himself by twisting or hurting her hand, her hold, from which eventually he frees himself (by cutting her). He thought that he had tried to set himself free from her influence in the past but had been unable to do so because he felt the need for her as a parent. Eventually he pours water over the fire, literally faced his grief at her loss and by so doing stamped out her emotional hold over him as was evidenced by the release of her captives (his encysted trauma). In session this was a major release of repressed feelings. He saw that when the witch went for his throat, this was symbolic of his feeling choked up, difficulty in speaking about how he felt. Yet, he had no wish to hit her, rather to hold her close to him. But daylight is dawning, he feels, and the former mother-image he had held of her is disappearing.

The journey back has obstacles on the path and the white horse is reluctant to go into the stable, or interpreted in the real life situation, the trauma of the break-up of his parents in his earlier years had brought problems, since he recognised that he tended to view relationships critically. On the one hand he accepted that he would like a pure relationship with a wife but had been disillusioned by the parental marriage. The stable in the Daydream represented a sort of stability of home life but in his case that is unbalanced because there is no woman, no mother, only his father there, so he is reluctant to return to an empty home.

He suspected that his mother might have formed an association with another man but he had found it difficult to ask her outright because he could not admit that she might have normal sexual appetites. He liked to retain his image of her as being pure. In like manner he admitted that he felt ashamed of the erotic images he had of women, regarding such thoughts as impure, below the ideal he held sacred. He recognised that he would be unable to make any new ground in his life until he was able to discuss things fully with his mother. This he eventually did and the subsequent release brought about improvements in his understanding and ability to communicate with other people much more easily.

His fourth Daydream he was able to translate as follows:-

"I had difficulty in reaching ground level which I believe to mean that I had no common ground with my own father. By hanging upside down I feel that this was a picture of my world being turned upside down when my father and mother separated. I wondered, when I sat on the horse and I still had something round my waist, whether this was symbolic of the umbilical cord that still linked me with my mother. The mouth of the wizard's cave being small I took to mean the difficulty in communicating with my father. The sealing of the cave around my horse was accompanied by a feeling of some suffocation during the Daydream and this probably is symbolic of the oppressiveness of living with my father after mother had left us. The thinness of the walls indicated that at any time I could have broken free but did not do so. As I now understand that movements in the Daydreams to the left are to do with the feminine side of things, whereas movements to the right are to do with the masculine, I believe the curve to the left denoted a tendency to prefer communication with my mother. The cave getting smaller and smaller made me think of my father who tends to hold himself in, making little effort to broaden out, which includes his relationship with me. The cave being "exactly oblong with a curved roof" told me that although I had some home stability, it is both limited and confining."

"What about the wizard's hat?"

"It was high and pointed and probably to do with my father's attitude, aloof and communication being confined to a point".

"Could you explain that?"

"Well, he limits his conversation to the immediate replies and makes no attempt to *talk to me*". The subsequent tricks of the wizard such as changing into a pterodactyl, spinning around, etc., Stuart thought were due to his father's going around in circles, literally getting nowhere. The wizard's long nails were, he thought, symbolic of scratching at things but never really getting to grips with life. He said that his father never seemed to profit from his mistakes, failed to adapt to change and to make progress. The difficulty in removing the wizard's hat he translated as meaning difficulty in his getting through to him to bring about a change of attitude. The cutting in various directions symbolised, for him, his attempts to get through to his father as there was always the risk that his father might 'fly off the handle' that is, get angry with him or sever the already tenuous hold on their relationship. Stuart decided that perhaps a new approach was needed. He said that he had successfully come to terms with the relationship inasmuch as he no longer condemned his father but could accept him for what he is.

Coming to terms with Societal constraints in the fifth Daydream, he saw that his being blown out of the dragon's cave was the rebuffs he had already experienced in his life. Cutting off its tail (the sting which could still wriggle) indicated that he could still be upset by societal constraints. When he cut the dragon in two and both his parents emerged, he believed that to be symbolically releasing them, freeing, or coming to terms with the emotional impact they had caused him. Since the previous Daydreams he had spoken frankly to both his parents, explaining how he had been affected by their separation. The pat on the back his father gave him in the Daydream symbolised his having earned his father's praise, that is, by verbalising his feelings or communicating them, which his father could never have done. Both parents encouraged him in his fight with the dragon, a recognition that in spite of everything each of them within their limitations does wish him to succeed in life. When the dragon's tail shrunk to half its former size it was because the problem had diminished. Turning all this over he said that he had achieved an *emotional* victory that he found it difficult to rationalise on an analytical level. Whatever had been holding him back in life was being released.

The final Daydream, when he was pushed out of the room, he related to his real-life situation at work. It seems he had felt that he had been pushed out of his rightful place, that is, passed over by his employers when he should have been promoted. However, this was but a temporary setback for he had gone back into the fight and had taken steps in his real-life situation to make a new career for himself in accountancy for which he had a flair. He realised that although the dragon (society) appeared to be asleep, it needed watching because things were not always what they seemed on the surface. He recognised that he had the ability to see things more clearly, however. The symbolism of the changing of the desert to being fertile instead of barren showed him that he had it within him to create changes in his life.

His winning of the princess pleased him because he said that she represented a woman *other* than his mother, whose image had dominated him. He saw his own need to take part in activities of a social and possibly religious nature, in which he had discovered a genuine interest since working through the Daydreams. He said that he no longer felt depressed or introspective and believed that he was now quite capable of meeting and communicating with others, including girls, and that he looked forward to his future and the experiences which were ahead of him in his life.

*   *   *

CHAPTER 12

I promised in Chapter 5 to give an illustration, written entirely in verse by one of my clients, to provide an example of what Desoille describes as "an extraordinary richness of imagery in certain especially talented subjects". Alas, I am able only to partially keep my promise for when I came to copy out the verses I discovered that many of them were missing and after a really thorough search of my files I can only conclude that the missing verses were accidentally destroyed when I was clearing out papers recently.

However, the verses that I have retained are reproduced below. If my client should happen to read this book and has kept a copy of her verses herself, I would be delighted to have the missing verses and will reimburse the cost of printing and postage!

"I stood in a sea of rippling green
And skyward did turn my face;
The midsummer sun smiled down on me -
I welcomed its warm embrace.
And high in that sky of azure blue
Were whispers of cloudy white,
Which some unseen artist's subtle stroke
Had painted for my delight.
My feet found a pathway through the lea,
I let them lead where they would,
'Til at my left hand, in grand array,
A forest of green oaks stood.
The trees were as tall and straight and proud
As pillars in marble hall,
With branches entwined like link-ed arms
Each wrapped in a leafy shawl.
I followed the footpath's gentle slope
Down into a verdant vale,
Where on either side were slumbering hills
Like giants of ancient tale.
Far off in the distance, mountains rose
Majestic to craggy peak,
All cloaked in a purple heather-hue
And snow-capped they were. and bleak.
At length to the mountain's foot I came,
Whence upward I sought a way
But sheer and forbidding was its face
And bitter was my dismay.
Then out of the distant hills there raced
As swift as an eagle's wing,
As royal a steed as ever graced
The stables of any king.

His eyes were like fire, his coat did shine
Like silver beneath the sun;
He lifted his regal head and called
To me as I watched him run.
Then onto his back he bade me climb
His pinions he did unfold.
He bore me in circles upward, as
In legend that once was told.
We looked down from the mountain's lofty peak
Down onto the scene below
Where valley and hillside, wood and field
Were bathed in a golden glow.
As thus we both stood in reverie,
Strange clouds gathered overhead
And down to the summit, from these clouds
A magical staircase led.
My heart stirred within me and my feet
Made haste to begin the climb,
As if a fond voice had called to me
Far down through the mists of time.
I mounted the staircase, step by step
And then to my wondering eyes,
A figure appeared to welcome me
From out of those azure skies.
She was clothed in a gown of emerald
That billowed about her feet.
Rich russet her hair, milk-white her skin;
Her voice it was soft and sweet.
She shone with the radiance of a star,
This lady of wondrous grace;
The tears sprang unbidden to my eyes,
For I gazed on my Mother's face.
She gave me a cup into my hands -
A chalice of silver fine:
'Twas wrought all about with ivy leaves
And filled with a rich, red wine.
A magical cup it was, she said;
The wine it would never spill
And nothing of evil need I fear
While the cup I had by me still.
I raised it aloft in silent pledge -
It glowed with a silver light
I thought that its lovely, lustrous sheen
Would lighten the darkest night.
Then into my hands she gave a scroll
Of parchment with silver bound;
This too was uncommon mystical
As to my surprise I found.

For when in much haste I opened it,
No lettering could I find.
It seemed my impatient, searching eyes
The scroll had the power to blind.
Yet when with care the page I unfurled
And read but its opening line
The letters were clear and boldly made
As though by a scribe most fine.
"Go down from the mountain, child". I read,
"For there will begin your quest".
I turned with a slow, unwilling step
To follow the scroll's behest.
The great winged horse could not be found;
I called to him, but in vain.
Then spied him far off in the distant hills
And prayed we might meet again.
I searched for the safest, surest way
To come to the mountain's base
And happened upon a length of rope
Conveniently tied in place.
The rope it was light as gossamer.
As smooth as a silken strand,
It lowered me with the greatest ease
To level and grassy land
Retracing my steps, I made my way
Through valley and over lea,
'Til I came at last to a steep cliff's edge
And looked down upon the sea.
A tortuous, snaking pathway wound
To an outcrop of rock below.
I slithered on scree and scrubby grass
My progress was hard and slow.
I rested upon my rocky shelf,
Refreshed by the sea's salt spray.
The crash of the waves and gulls' harsh cries
Made music most wild and fey.

These verses on Desoille's Directed Daydreams serve as a classic example of the unfolding of imagination by a young lady whose life certainly took on new dimensions after her therapy sessions.

Appendix 1

A Classic Illustration of How the Mind Can Affect the Body

The following case history originally appeared in *Appendix Three* to my report, *Analysis of Psychotherapy, Hypnotherapy and Orthomolecular Therapy treatments carried out between 1974* and *1982 in* **England,** *Canada and the United States*, submitted to the British Medical Association in September 1983. It is a classic illustration of how the mind can affect the bodily functions. It also serves to demonstrate the effectiveness of Freud's *Free Association*, one of the techniques used in psychotherapy.

Mr. D., aged 49, married with 2 sons and 2 daughters; youngest daughter aged 9 still living at home but all the older children married. Mr. D's occupation is a factory worker.

Presenting symptoms:

Very painful left shoulder causing inability to raise his left arm above shoulder height with consequent difficulty in dressing himself and in performing some of his duties at the factory where he is employed. Onset one year prior to his seeking psychotherapy, following a fall at the factory whilst hosing down the floor. He had sought treatment to alleviate the condition from both orthodox and complementary practitioners but with little or no improvement. This had included physiotherapy in which he had himself worked and was consequently well versed in the techniques of relaxation although the painful shoulder had failed to respond to "everything tried".

Free Association technique was used, following the initial consultation during which I worked through the completion of a word association test with him. I noticed from this test that although he was able to relax throughout, there had been a very perceptible movement (a convulsive jerky movement forward) which gave pointers to the possible area where his problem might have arisen and made me decide to proceed with the Free Association technique. During the first session he was asked to describe in detail the incident where he fell on the factory floor. His recollection of this incident was extremely good and he was able to describe in detail the whole episode from the time he tripped against the base of a heavy piece of machinery, lost his balance and fell heavily on his left side, injuring his knee and left shoulder. He described the machine as being "a smoke-grey sort of gun-metal colour". He also described how he had massaged his swollen knee and brought the swelling down very rapidly by working on an acupressure point (he had studied and practised acupuncture with his family and friends) and had proceeded to work with his right hand massaging his left shoulder as best he could and applying pressure to the acupressure point. However, the shoulder had failed to respond and he had been troubled with it ever since. He was encouraged to free float to other disturbing incidents in his life but these appeared to have no relation to his present problem. A further appointment was made by him for the following week.

He arrived punctually for his appointment the following week. The incident on the factory floor was gone through again and following this he was asked to recall the first time he had suffered a really painful shoulder. He was silent for a few moments and then began to describe an incident when he was serving as a Despatch Rider in Germany in 1945. It was obvious that he was really "into" this incident and was encouraged to describe it fully as he relived it. He proceeded to describe an accident where he was involved in a collision with a German lorry that appeared suddenly in front of him, shooting out of a side road onto the main highway. He described the road as being wet (as it was raining slightly at the time) and he had apparently no time to apply the brakes of his motor cycle and drove straight into the lorry. He recalled that he was travelling about 40 m.p.h. and that on impact he felt a sudden jarring throughout his body, a feeling as if his body was coming apart. He blacked out and remembered coming to and seeing a lot of faces "upside down but above" him which made him feel bewildered at first. However, as he became more aware he recalled the impact, which was confirmed by the sight of his helmet that had a large dent in it, and which he assumed had been caused by his being precipitated forward on impact. No bones had been broken and he was able to resume duty the following day after being examined by the Medical Officer although he was still feeling rather shaken up and aching.

During his recall of the incident he described the German lorry as being of a smoke-grey, gun-metal colour and that the morning after the accident he had awoken with a very stiff and painful shoulder. It did not take long for him to find other connecting similarities with the later factory fall which had obviously restimulated this in his memory - the lorry and the machine were of identical colour; both were unyielding on impact; the sensation of being precipitated forward; inability to control his body; the road and factory floor both being wet; the smell of oil.

Following the reliving of these two incidents he was able to lift his left arm way above his head when asked to do so. He subsequently was delighted to demonstrate that he could remove and replace his jacket without pain.

The two incidents were thirty years apart!

Appendix 2

The following case history appeared in Appendix C to my report, *Analysis of Psychotherapy and Orthomolecular Therapy treatments carried out between 1987 and 1988 in England,* submitted to the British Medical Association in May, 1988.

Marion, a married woman with three grown up sons and a grown up daughter, was fifty years old when she first sought psychotherapy.

Presenting symptoms: Agoraphobia, vertigo and palpitations.

Health History: showed measles and mumps at ages 5 and 6, German measles at 31, Chicken Pox at 33, Glandular Fever at 35 and onset of Agoraphobia, Vertigo and Palpitations at age 36. Treatment had comprised fourteen different tranquillisers, the last being *Ativan*, over the fourteen years prior to therapy, none of which had been of any real benefit.

At the initial consultation various tests were carried out indicating that Marion had no minimal brain damage, was above average intelligence and had a low score stress rating.

Hypnosis was suggested to which she raised no objection and an eye-to-eye induction method was used as Marion had some difficulty in not averting her eyes during conversation. After the induction her left index finger was placed under the control of her deeper consciousness and was used as the idiomotor signal. This clearly indicated that her original problem arose when she was two years of age but that another situation when she was 33 had an important bearing on the problem. There was also a signal that something had happened at age 42 which had caused a similar feeling of loss of security. Before bring her out of the hypnotic state the suggestion was implanted that as she had discovered that there was a reason for the problems she had suffered which would be dealt with at subsequent sessions there was no need for her to feel anxious about them and, at the next session when she heard me count backwards three, two, one, then her eyes are closing, her body relaxing, and she is going into even deeper relaxation.

The next consultation was nearly a fortnight later but during that fortnight she had enjoyed a feeling of well-being and there had been no problems with palpitations. Hypnosis was achieved rapidly and she was directed back to age 2. The incident she relived was when she was with her mother in a crowded department store and took hold of the skirt of someone else believing she was holding her mother's skirt and actually left the store with the other woman. During the reliving of the incident there was an excellent release of emotion with deep sobbing followed by hysterical screaming. The incident ended on a happy note with her mother being reunited with her. Marion was then directed to move through the years to age 33. The second incident concerned the burglary of her parental home, the trauma it caused her parents, and her own reluctance to face going into the house as it seemed like a violation of her own memories of a happy home life. Eventually she forced herself to go there but felt that she had to keep her gloves on so that she did not come into contact with anything the robbers might have touched. The incident at age 42 was when her only daughter left home. Under hypnosis Marion was directed to the very first time she had experienced Agoraphobia and dizziness - it was when she had been shopping in a busy store and she had had to get outside into the air and just wanted to get home but had to queue up at a bus stop and she was overcome by dizziness while she had to stand and wait for the bus. The idiomotor signal indicated that the incidents relevant to her problem had been completed. An appointment was made for the following week.

When she arrived for her third consultation she told me that she had gone out during the week, even attending a function alone and was very pleased with her progress, feeling that she had accomplished something for the first time in fourteen years. At this consultation I suggested the use of the Directed Daydream method to which she agreed.

Following the successful completion of Daydream One she had not only been out alone many times but had also climbed up into the loft of her house and cleared it out getting back down unaided. She told me that her husband and her family had been amazed because long ago she had climbed the ladder into the loft but was too fearful to get down and stayed there terrified and trembling for ages. Finally, it seems, help had been summoned but once down on that occasion she thought that she would never again be able to climb up there!

At the conclusion of the six day-dreams she had no longer any fear of going out, had lost the feelings of vertigo and dizziness and was leading a very active life again.

After psychotherapy was terminated I received a letter from her husband, which reads:

> "Just a line to express my gratitude for all that you have achieved with Marion. Few can imagine or understand the torments she had suffered for well over a decade - the frustration and desperation of making no real progress and the seeming indifference of "specialists". All that has now changed - optimism is again part of her life and, as I write this letter, she is studying brochures and deciding where to go for a holiday; I pray that you will continue to help others as you have helped Marion. May God be forever by your side."

The effectiveness of the Desoille method can be further illustrated with hundreds, if not thousands, of other case histories; it works extremely well with phobic problems, inferiority complexes, emotional problems, etc., because it enables the clients to verbalise pictorially their fears and anxieties so well. Indeed, Hypnosis, the Free Association technique and Desoille's Daydreams are all valuable in bringing repressions out with full emotional releases. All these techniques can erase the basic causes of the problems suffered without the need for tranquillisers. The services of a trained psychotherapist should be available to the general public under the National Health Service, working in a close association with the General Practitioner or Psychiatric unit.

The author of this book is editor of *The Seeker*, a private subscription magazine published quarterly. *The Seeker* is dedicated to the search for truth and the publication of any information coming to light which carries us all that step further in our quest. It welcomes articles from those who can contribute new or rediscovered knowledge that can be of value to us all, fellow seekers, in our journey through life. The annual subscription in the U.K. is £12.50, £17.50 for overseas, including p/p. *(Correct at time of going to press)*

Enquiries should be sent to:
'Badger's Brook', 4 Brook Edge, Moor Lane, Brighstone,
Isle of Wight. PO 30 4DP

A complimentary copy of the first issue of the magazine will be sent on request, subject to availability but please enclose a self-addressed A.5 size envelope bearing appropriate postage stamps for up to 100g. Requests outside the U.K. please send three international reply coupons.

The logo for *The Seeker* is intended to depict man in his higher aspirations, his *potential of becoming* - becoming far more than the physical or material man to which he has been bound in the past. He sits astride the winged horse, ascending from his former Earthly limitations. The symbolism further portrays the inherent power of his *intent*, the power of his one true desire to rise in spirit above the restrictions that he may have formerly accepted and suffered.

Symbolism belongs to the world of archetypes and expresses a truth in a way that mere words cannot possibly convey. To hear the national anthem played when one is far from one's homeland is an example of the power of symbolism, for at that moment of recognition and identification is summarised all that our homeland means to us. Carl Jung in his book, *Man and his symbols*, has this to say of symbols of transcendence: "... these symbols do not seek to integrate the initiate with any religious doctrine or secular group-consciousness. On the contrary, they (highlight) man's need for liberation from any state of being that is too immature, too fixed or final. ... They concern man's release from, or transcendence of, any confining pattern of existence, as he moves toward a superior or more mature stage in his development."

Thus we have the true Seeker that dwells within each and every one of us.